P9-CSZ-757

1st EDITION

Perspectives on Diseases and Disorders

Parkinson's Disease

Carrie Fredericks
Book Editor

Detroit • New York • San Francisco • New Haven, Conn • Waterville, Maine • London

Christine Nasso, *Publisher*
Elizabeth Des Chenes, *Managing Editor*

© 2009 Greenhaven Press, a part of Gale, Cengage Learning

Gale and Greenhaven Press are registered trademarks used herein under license.

For more information, contact:
Greenhaven Press
27500 Drake Rd.
Farmington Hills, MI 48331-3535
Or you can visit our Internet site at gale.cengage.com

For product information and technology assistance, contact us at

Gale Customer Support, 1-800-877-4253
For permission to use material from this text or product, submit all requests online at www.cengage.com/permissions

Further permissions questions can be emailed to permissionrequest@cengage.com

Articles in Greenhaven Press anthologies are often edited for length to meet page requirements. In addition, original titles of these works are changed to clearly present the main thesis and to explicitly indicate the author's opinion. Every effort is made to ensure that Greenhaven Press accurately reflects the original intent of the authors. Every effort has been made to trace the owners of copyrighted material.

Cover image Jamie McCarthy/WireImage for The Michael J. Fox Foundation/Getty Images

LIBRARY OF CONGRESS CATALOGING-IN-PUBLICATION DATA

Parkinson's disease / Carrie Fredericks, book editor.
   p. cm. -- (Perspectives on diseases and disorders)
   Includes bibliographical references and index.
   ISBN 978-0-7377-4382-1 (hardcover)
   1. Parkinson's disease--Juvenile literature.
   RC382.P37 2009
   616.8'33--dc22

                                                2009002455

Printed in the United States of America
1 2 3 4 5 6 7 13 12 11 10 09

CONTENTS

gene therapy, environmental toxins, cell systems, biomarkers, alternative treatments, and cell therapy.

CHAPTER 2   The Controversial Side of Parkinson's

CHAPTER 3   The Personal Side of Parkinson's

FOREWORD

"Medicine, to produce health, has to examine disease."
—Plutarch

Independent research on a health issue is often the first step to complement discussions with a physician. But locating accurate, well-organized, understandable medical information can be a challenge. A simple Internet search on terms such as "cancer" or "diabetes," for example, returns an intimidating number of results. Sifting through the results can be daunting, particularly when some of the information is inconsistent or even contradictory. The Greenhaven Press series Perspectives on Diseases and Disorders offers a solution to the often overwhelming nature of researching diseases and disorders.

From the clinical to the personal, titles in the Perspectives on Diseases and Disorders series provide student and other researchers with authoritative, accessible information in unique anthologies that include basic information about the disease or disorder, controversial aspects of diagnosis and treatment, and first-person accounts of those impacted by the disease. The result is a well-rounded combination of primary and secondary sources that, together, provide the reader with a better understanding of the disease or disorder.

Each volume in Perspectives on Diseases and Disorders explores a particular disease or disorder in detail. Material for each volume is carefully selected from a wide range of sources, including encyclopedias, journals, newspapers, nonfiction books, speeches, government documents, pamphlets, organization newsletters, and position papers. Articles in the first chapter provide an authoritative, up-to-date overview that covers symptoms, causes and effects, treatments, cures, and medical advances. The second chapter presents a substantial number of opposing viewpoints on controversial treatments and other current debates relating to the volume topic. The third chapter offers a variety of personal perspectives on the disease or disorder. Patients, doctors, caregivers, and loved ones represent just some of the voices found in this narrative chapter.

Each Perspectives on Diseases and Disorders volume also includes:

- An **annotated table of contents** that provides a brief summary of each article in the volume.
- An **introduction** specific to the volume topic.
- Full-color **charts and graphs** to illustrate key points, concepts, and theories.
- Full-color **photos** that show aspects of the disease or disorder and enhance textual material.
- **"Fast Facts"** that highlight pertinent additional statistics and surprising points.
- A **glossary** providing users with definitions of important terms.
- A **chronology** of important dates relating to the disease or disorder.
- An annotated list of **organizations to contact** for students and other readers seeking additional information.
- A **bibliography** of additional books and periodicals for further research.
- A detailed **subject index** that allows readers to quickly find the information they need.

Whether a student researching a disorder, a patient recently diagnosed with a disease, or an individual who simply wants to learn more about a particular disease or disorder, a reader who turns to Perspectives on Diseases and Disorders will find a wealth of information in each volume that offers not only basic information, but also vigorous debate from multiple perspectives.

INTRODUCTION

For thousands of years people have dealt with Parkinson's disease. More than seven thousand years ago, Parkinson's-like symptoms were described in an ancient Indian text. Over four hundred years ago, in the play *The Second Part of King Henry the Sixth*, William Shakespeare created a character who has a shaking palsy, the name used at that time for Parkinson's disease. Over the centuries this condition has become more widespread, with more scientific information being discovered about it every day. Parkinson's also ranks among the

There are five stages of Parkinson's disease. In stage four the patient requires assistance and is no longer able to live alone. (**David Leah/ Photo Researchers, Inc.**)

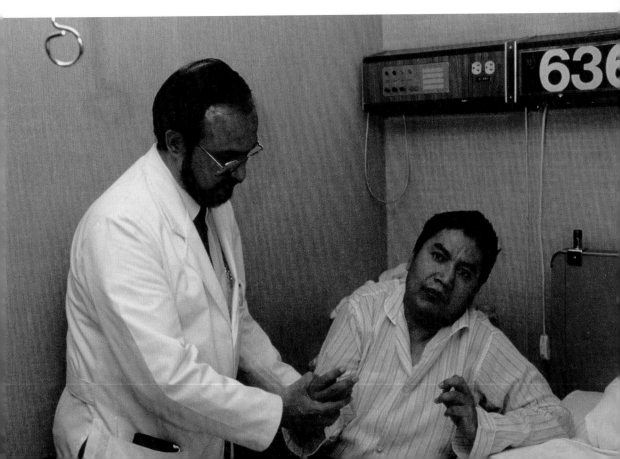

most devastating diseases. In October 2007, *Popular Science* magazine labeled it one of the "Deadly Five: . . . the biggest, scariest enemies of the brain."[1] There are great physical and emotional tolls that come from this incurable disease, and the five stages of Parkinson's give good examples of the hurdles patients face. In 1967 physicians M.M. Hoehn and M.D. Yahr developed a scale that distinguished five distinct stages of Parkinson's, each one with its own challenges. According to the California-based Parkinson's Resource Organization, "These stages can take anywhere from four years to forty years. The differences depend on the person with the diagnosis."[2] Parkinson's symptoms vary widely in severity and frequency, and skipping stages is not altogether uncommon.

Stage one is called early onset, or initial, Parkinson's. Symptoms are usually mild and occur on one side of the body. These symptoms often include tremor or shaking in one limb and small changes in posture, movement, and facial expressions. While inconvenient, this stage is not disabling in any way and may last for many years. Medication is generally used to try to halt further harm to the nervous system.

Stage two is the bilateral stage. Symptoms appear on both sides of the body and affect both limbs. In stage two, minor disability becomes apparent, with posture and gait affected. While some patients skip this stage, patients are classified as being in stage two even if the symptoms appearing on the second side occur very infrequently. Medications known as dopamine agonists have recently begun being used in this stage. Researchers say that using these medications at this stage may help prevent some of the more difficult side effects that result from use of these drugs during later stages of the disease.

Stage three is often called moderate Parkinson's. The disease has progressed far enough that a patient may have difficulty maintaining posture and body position. Balance is affected when a person walks or stands, and falling down can be common; there is also significant slowing of body movements. In this stage, medication on-off cycles (times when a medication is more or less effective) begin, but this is usually predictable. A stage three patient can still maintain his or her independence.

Stage four is advanced Parkinson's. A patient in this stage requires considerable help and is no longer able to live alone. Balance problems increase at this stage, and falling down becomes much more common. Rigidity and slowing of body movements is very apparent, but tremor may subside to some extent. Some patients have surgery during this stage to help alleviate a number of the more problematic symptoms, but this is usually limited to those who are somewhat younger and are in otherwise good health.

Stage five indicates severe Parkinson's. It is often called the end stage. This stage requires the patient to have constant nursing care because patients are restricted to a wheelchair or bed and can only walk with assistance. At this stage, people begin to have atrophy of muscle mass resulting from the accelerated disuse of muscles for walking and other everyday tasks. Surgery may be an option in this stage, including pallidotomy and deep brain stimulation, but medications are still used to help the patient control as many symptoms as possible.

The five stages of Parkinson's make it clear that this disease takes a great toll on the body over the course of time. But in addition to the rigors of the disease itself, emotional upheaval often accompanies the clinical symptoms. One of the main mental disorders associated with Parkinson's is depression. In a July 30, 2008, *New York Times* article, movement disorder neurologist Irene Richard states, "Research has shown us that in some cases, depression may be the first sign of Parkinson's disease, appearing well before any motor symptoms, and so we think it may be part of the underlying disease process."[3]

According to research statistics, up to 40 percent of Parkinson's patients develop depression. But depression

In an effort to find a cure for Parkinson's, longtime sufferers of the disease Muhammad Ali and Michael J. Fox testify before Congress on the need for increased funding to find a cure. (Chris Corder/UPI/Landov)

in these patients is not always the same as in people without Parkinson's disease. With Parkinson's disease the severity of the depression is not related to the severity of the disease. In the same article, Richard explains, "Not everyone who has Parkinson's gets depressed, so there's probably something going on that makes certain people vulnerable and others not—and this vulnerability doesn't seem to be related to the severity of the disease or how disabled the person is. So a person with mild Parkinson's symptoms might become severely depressed, whereas someone with worse symptoms doesn't."[4]

One of the main concerns with depression in Parkinson's patients is the ability to administer antidepressants. Because Parkinson's is a brain disease, there is no way to know if these types of antidepressant medications will work as well in Parkinson's patients as they do in people without the disease. Also, Parkinson's patients are usually on a number of other medications and it is difficult to know if these will interfere with the effectiveness of the antidepressants or cause side effects that would not be seen in non-Parkinson's patients.

Hallucinations are also associated with Parkinson's disease. Some Parkinson's medications are known to cause auditory and visual illusions or hallucinations. Illusions are formed from external stimuli while hallucinations are formed within a person's mind regardless of what is happening around him or her. In the *New York Times* article "Marilyn and Me: Dealing with Illusions (or Life on a Parkinson's Drug)," author and Parkinson's patient Mark Derr writes, "The vast majority of hallucinations are visual. Of the 10 to 12 percent of patients who have auditory hallucinations, only about 2 percent hear sound alone. Tactile and taste hallucinations are more rare but are not unknown."[5]

The cause of these illusions and hallucinations is not currently known. Some researchers believe that they are caused only by the medications, while others argue that the disease itself may be the underlying cause. It has been suggested that roughly 40 percent of Parkinson's patients suffer some form of illusions or hallucinations. But not much in-depth study has been conducted on this aspect of the disease.

While the disease stages and emotional tolls of Parkinson's can be overwhelming, hope is always present that a cure will be found. As genetic and molecular biology becomes more and more sophisticated and precise, the chances for a major breakthrough become greater. In an October 2006 interview with Katie Couric, actor Michael J. Fox spoke about hope for the future: "I had dinner, lunch with a 17 year old girl from Ohio, who has Parkinson's, and is very symptomatic. She'll be in her early 30's in 15 years, and I don't think she'd write that off as a long time. I think if we can tell her . . . that we'd have an answer for her in 15 years, I don't think she'd treat that lightly. I think that would give her strength and hope to hang on."[6]

Notes

1. Eric Hagerman, "The Deadly Five," *Popular Science*, vol. 271, no. 4, October 2007.
2. Jo Rosen, "Presidents Message," Parkinson's Resource Organization, September 7, 2006. www.parkinsonsresource.org.
3. Quoted in Marilynn Larkin, "The Emotional Toll of Parkinson's Disease," *New York Times*, July 30, 2008. http://health.nytimes.com.
4. Quoted in Larkin, "The Emotional Toll of Parkinson's Disease."
5. Mark Derr, "Marilyn and Me: Dealing with Illusions (or Life on a Parkinson's Drug)," *New York Times*, February 14, 2006. www.nytimes.com/2006/02/14/health/14case.html.
6. "Transcript: Michael J. Fox," *CBS Evening News with Katie Couric*, October 26, 2006. www.cbsnews.com/stories/2006/10/26/evening news/main2129702.shtml.

CHAPTER 1

Understanding Parkinson's Disease

An Overview of Parkinson's

Laith Farid Gulli and Ken R. Wells

In the following viewpoint Laith Farid Gulli and Ken R. Wells provide an overview of Parkinson's disease, covering its causes, symptoms, treatment, and prognosis. Ultimately, Parkinson's affects the movement control center in the brain, the authors explain, and since the symptoms affect every person at a different rate, treatments are usually individualized for every Parkinson's case. Alternative treatments for relieving Parkinson's symptoms and helping with muscle control are becoming more widely used. However, say the authors, the prognosis for Parkinson's remains grim; while research strides are being made, the disease itself still worsens over time. Gulli is a Michigan-based psychotherapist. Wells is a science and business writer.

Photo on previous page. A scientist studies stem cells as part of research to develop cell therapies for Parkinson's disease. (Javier Soriano/AFP/ Getty Images)

P arkinson disease (PD) is a progressive movement disorder marked by tremors, rigidity, slow movements (bradykinesia), and posture instability. It occurs when cells in one of the movement-control cen-

SOURCE: Laith Farid Gulli and Ken R. Wells, "Parkinson Disease," *The Gale Encyclopedia of Medicine.* Detroit: Gale, 2007. Reproduced by permission of Gale, a part of Cengage Learning.

ters of the brain begin to die for unknown reasons. PD was first noted by British physician James Parkinson in the early 1800s.

Usually beginning in a person's late fifties or early sixties, Parkinson disease causes a progressive decline in movement control, affecting the ability to control initiation, speed, and smoothness of motion. Symptoms of PD are seen in up to 15% of those ages 65–74, and almost 30% of those ages 75–84.

The Stages of Parkinson's Disease

Stage 0	No sign of disease
Stage 1	Unilateral disease (affecting either left or right side of the body); symptoms mild
Stage 1.5	Unilateral disease and axial (neck and back/trunk)
Stage 2	Mild bilateral (left and right) disease, without impairment of balance
Stage 2.5	Mild bilateral disease, with some mild imbalance
Stage 3	Mild to moderate bilateral disease with some difficulty with balance; still physically independent
Stage 4	Moderate to severe bilateral disease with marked disability (needs help with most daily motor tasks such as dressing, bathing, eating); still able to walk or stand without a person assisting, but may need a cane or walker; unable to live alone
Stage 5	Advanced disease, wheelchair bound or bedridden; requires nursing care; may experience malnutrition

Taken from: Gretchen Garie and Michael J. Church, *Living Well with Parkinson's Disease: What Your Doctor Doesn't Tell You . . . That You Need to Know.* New York: Collins, 2007.

Most cases of PD are sporadic. This means that there is a spontaneous and permanent change in nucleotide sequences (the building blocks of genes). Sporadic mutations also involve unknown environmental factors in combination with genetic defects. The abnormal gene (mutated gene) will form an altered end-product or protein. This will cause abnormalities in specific areas in the body where the protein is used. Some evidence suggests that the disease is transmitted by autosomal dominant inheritance. This implies that an affected parent has a 50% chance of transmitting the disease to any child. This type of inheritance is not commonly observed. The most recent evidence is linking PD with a gene that codes for a protein called alpha-synuclein. Further research is attempting to fully understand the relationship with this protein and nerve cell degeneration.

PD affects approximately 1.5 million people in the United States, both men and women, with as many as 50,000 new cases each year.

The Suspected Causes of Parkinson's

The immediate cause of PD is degeneration of brain cells in the area known as the substantia nigra, one of the movement control centers of the brain. Damage to this area leads to the cluster of symptoms known as "parkinsonism." In PD, degenerating brain cells contain Lewy bodies, which help identify the disease. The cell death leading to parkinsonism may be caused by a number of conditions, including infection, trauma, and poisoning. Some drugs given for psychosis, such as haloperidol (Haldol) or chlorpromazine (thorazine), may cause parkinsonism. When no cause for nigral cell degeneration can be found, the disorder is called idiopathic parkinsonism, or Parkinson disease. Parkinsonism may be seen in other degenerative conditions, known as the "parkinsonism plus" syndromes, such as progressive supranuclear palsy.

The substantia nigra, or "black substance," is one of the principal movement control centers in the brain. By releasing the neurotransmitter known as dopamine, it helps to refine movement patterns throughout the body. The dopamine released by nerve cells of substantia nigra stimulates another brain region, the corpus striatum. Without enough dopamine, the corpus striatum cannot control its targets, and so on down the line. Ultimately, the movement patterns of walking, writing, reaching for objects, and other basic programs cannot operate properly, and the symptoms of parkinsonism are the result.

There are some known toxins that can cause parkinsonism, most notoriously a chemical called MPTP, found as an impurity in some illegal drugs. Parkinsonian symptoms appear within hours of ingestion, and are permanent. MPTP may exert its effects through generation of toxic molecular fragments called free radicals, and reducing free radicals has been a target of several experimental treatments for PD using antioxidants.

It is possible that early exposure to some as-yet-unidentified environmental toxin or virus leads to undetected nigral cell death, and PD then manifests as normal age-related decline brings the number of functioning nigral cells below the threshold needed for normal movement. It is also possible that, for genetic reasons, some people are simply born with fewer cells in their substantia nigra than others, and they develop PD as a consequence of normal decline.

PD's Primary Symptoms Relate to Movement

The identifying symptoms of PD include:

• Tremors, usually beginning in the hands, often occurring on one side before the other. The classic tremor of PD is called a "pill-rolling tremor," because the movement resembles rolling a pill between the thumb and forefinger. This tremor occurs at a frequency of about three per second.

- Slow movements (bradykinesia) occur, which may involve slowing down or stopping in the middle of familiar tasks such as walking, eating, or shaving. This may include freezing in place during movements (akinesia).
- Muscle rigidity or stiffness, occurring with jerky movements replacing smooth motion.
- Postural instability or balance difficulty occurs. This may lead to a rapid, shuffling gait (festination) to prevent falling.
- In most cases, there is a "masked face," with little facial expression and decreased eye-blinking.

In addition, a wide range of other symptoms may often be seen, some beginning earlier than others:

- depression
- speech changes, including rapid speech without inflection changes
- problems with sleep, including restlessness and nightmares
- emotional changes, including fear, irritability, and insecurity
- incontinence
- constipation
- handwriting changes, with letters becoming smaller across the page (micrographia)
- progressive problems with intellectual function (dementia)

The Diagnosis and Treatment Options

The diagnosis of Parkinson disease involves a careful medical history and a neurological exam to look for characteristic symptoms. There are no definitive tests for PD, although a variety of lab tests may be done to rule out other causes of symptoms, especially if only some of the identifying symptoms are present. Tests for other causes of parkinsonism may include brain scans, blood tests, lumbar puncture, and x rays.

There is no cure for Parkinson disease. Most drugs treat the symptoms of the disease only, although one drug, selegiline (Eldepryl), may slow degeneration of the substantia nigra.

Regular, moderate exercise has been shown to improve motor function without an increase in medication for a person with PD. Exercise helps maintain range of motion in stiff muscles, improve circulation, and stimulate appetite. An exercise program designed by a physical therapist has the best chance of meeting the specific needs of the person with PD. A physical therapist may also suggest strategies for balance compensation and techniques to stimulate movement during slowdowns or freezes.

Good nutrition is important to maintenance of general health. A person with PD may lose some interest in food, especially if depressed, and may have nausea from the disease or from medications, especially those known as dopamine agonists. Slow movements may make it difficult to eat quickly, and delayed gastric emptying may lead to a feeling of fullness without having eaten much. Increasing fiber in the diet can improve constipation, soft foods can reduce the amount of needed chewing, and a prokinetic drug can increase the movement of food through the digestive system.

People with PD may need to limit the amount of protein in their diets. The main drug used to treat PD, L-dopa, is an amino acid, and is absorbed by the digestive system by the same transporters that pick up other amino acids broken down from proteins in the diet. Limiting protein, under the direction of the physician or a nutritionist, can improve the absorption of L-dopa.

No evidence indicates that vitamin or mineral supplements can have any effect on the disease other than in the improvement of the patient's general health. No antioxidants used to date have shown promise as a treatment except for selegiline, an MAO-B inhibitor. . . . A large, carefully controlled study of vitamin E demonstrated that it could not halt disease progression.

The Right Drug Depends on the Patient

The pharmacological treatment of Parkinson disease is complex. While there are a large number of drugs that can be effective, their effectiveness varies with the patient, disease progression, and the length of time the drug has been used. Dose-related side effects may preclude using the most effective dose, or require the introduction of a new drug to counteract them. There are six classes of drugs currently used to treat PD.

Drugs that replace dopamine. One drug that helps replace dopamine, levodopa (L-dopa), is the single most effective treatment for the symptoms of PD. L-dopa is a derivative of dopamine, and is converted into dopamine by the brain. It may be started when symptoms begin, or when they become serious enough to interfere with work or daily living.

L-dopa therapy usually remains effective for five years or longer. Following this, many patients develop motor fluctuations, including peak-dose "dyskinesias" (abnormal movements such as tics, twisting, or restlessness), rapid loss of response after dosing (known as the "on-off" phenomenon), and unpredictable drug response. Higher doses are usually tried, but may lead to an increase in dyskinesias. In addition, side effects of L-dopa include nausea and vomiting, and low blood pressure upon standing (orthostatic hypotension), which can cause dizziness. These effects usually lessen after several weeks of therapy.

Enzyme inhibitors. Dopamine is broken down by several enzyme systems in the brain and elsewhere in the body, and blocking these enzymes is a key strategy to prolonging the effect of dopamine. The two most commonly prescribed forms of L-dopa contain a drug to inhibit the amino acid decarboxylase (an AADC inhibitor), one type of enzyme that breaks down dopamine. These combination drugs are Sinemet (L-dopa plus carbidopa) and Madopar (L-dopa plus benzaseride), Controlled-release formulations also aid in prolonging the effective interval of an L-dopa dose.

The enzyme monoamine oxidase B (MAO-B) inhibitor selegiline may be given as add-on therapy for L-dopa. Research indicates selegiline may have a neuroprotective effect, sparing nigral cells from damage by free radicals. Because of this, and the fact that it has few side effects, it is also frequently prescribed early in the disease before L-dopa is begun. Entacapone and tolcapone, two inhibitors of another enzyme system called catechol-o-methyl transferase (COMT), may soon reach the market as early studies suggest that they effectively treat PD symptoms with fewer motor fluctuations and decreased daily L-dopa requirements.

Cholinesterase inhibitors. The cholinesterase inhibitor Exelon (rivastigmine) both as a tablet and a transdermal patch is used to treat dementia in mild to moderate PD.

Dopamine agonists. Dopamine works by stimulating receptors on the surface of corpus striatum cells. Drugs that also stimulate these cells are called dopamine agonists, or DAs. DAs may be used before L-dopa therapy, or added on to avoid requirements for higher L-dopa doses late in the disease. DAs available in the United States as of 2007 include bromocriptine (Permax, Parlodel), ropinirole (Requip), and pramipexole (Mirapex). In 2007, the U.S. Food and Drug Administration (FDA) approved cabergoline (Dostinex) for treatment of PD. Other dopamine agonists in use elsewhere include lisuride (Dopergine) and apomorphine. Side effects of all the DAs are similar to those of dopamine, plus confusion and hallucinations at higher doses. In 2007, the drug pergolide (Permax) was withdrawn from sale in the United States and China after two studies showed it increased the risk of serious heart valve damage.

Anticholinergic drugs. Anticholinergics maintain dopamine balance as levels decrease. However, the side effects of anticholinergics (dry mouth, constipation, confusion, and blurred vision) are usually too severe in older patients or in patients with dementia. In addition, anticholinergics rarely work for very long. They are often prescribed for younger patients who have predominant shaking. Trihexyphenidyl (Artane) is the drug most commonly prescribed.

Drugs whose mode of action is uncertain. Amantadine (Symmetrel) is sometimes used as an early therapy before L-dopa is begun, and as an add-on later in the disease. Its anti-Parkinsonian effects are mild, and are not seen in many patients. Clozapine (Clozaril) is effective especially against psychiatric symptoms of late PD, including psychosis and hallucinations.

Surgical and Alternative Treatments

Two surgical procedures are used for treatment of PD that cannot be controlled adequately with drug therapy. In PD, a brain structure called the globus pallidus (GPi) receives excess stimulation from the corpus striatum. In a pallidotomy, the GPi is destroyed by heat, delivered by long thin needles inserted under anesthesia. Electrical stimulation of the GPi is another way to reduce its action. In this procedure, fine electrodes are inserted to deliver the stimulation, which may be adjusted or turned off as the response dictates. Other regions of the brain may also be stimulated by electrodes inserted elsewhere. In most patients, these procedures lead to significant improvement for some motor symptoms, including peak-dose dyskinesias. This allows the patient to receive more L-dopa, since these dyskinesias are usually what causes an upper limit on the L-dopa dose.

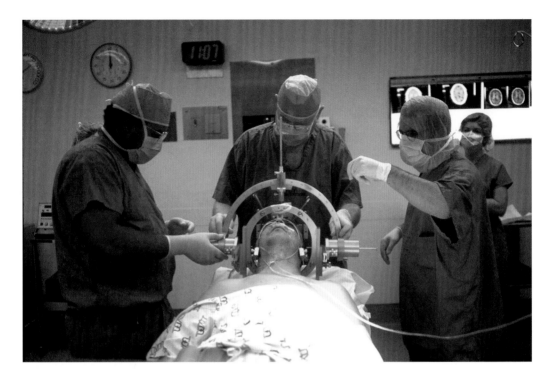

A third procedure, transplant of fetal nigral cells, is still highly experimental. Its benefits to date have been modest, although improvements in technique and patient selection are likely to change that. Also, as of 2007, gene therapy was showing promise as a future treatment for PD. In one trial by Cornell University scientists involving 12 patients with PD, all had their symptoms improved by at least 25% for up to a year after gene therapy. Further research was being conducted.

Currently, the best treatments for PD involve the use of conventional drugs such as levodopa. Alternative therapies, including acupuncture, massage, and yoga, can help relieve some symptoms of the disease and loosen tight muscles. Alternative practitioners have also applied herbal and dietary therapies, including amino acid supplementation, antioxidant (vitamins A, C, E, selenium, and zinc) therapy, B vitamin supplementation, and calcium and magnesium supplementation, to the treatment

Deep brain stimulation is performed on a patient. (© **Phototake Inc.**/Alamy)

of PD. Anyone using these therapies in conjunction with conventional drugs should check with their doctor to avoid the possibility of adverse interactions. For example, vitamin B6 (either as a supplement or from foods such as whole grains, bananas, beef, fish, liver, and potatoes) can interfere with the action of L-dopa when the drug is taken without carbidopa.

The Prognosis, with or Without Treatment

Despite medical treatment, the symptoms of Parkinson disease worsen over time, and become less responsive to drug therapy. Late-stage psychiatric symptoms are often the most troubling, including difficulty sleeping, nightmares, intellectual impairment (dementia), hallucinations, and loss of contact with reality (psychosis).

There is no known way to prevent Parkinson disease.

The Medicines
of Parkinson's

Nutan Sharma and Elaine Richman

Drug treatment of Parkinson's disease is undertaken mainly to help relieve symptoms, and there are six main classifications of medications for achieving this, according to Nutan Sharma and Elaine Richman. In the following viewpoint the authors discuss the different classes of medications and how they work; some block the effects of neurotransmitters, but most augment the release of dopamine or help stimulate dopamine receptors in the brain. By maintaining a set schedule of medication dosing, a patient is much more likely to control his or her symptoms, depending on how advanced the disease has become. Sharma is an assistant in neurology at Massachusetts General Hospital and an instructor at Harvard Medical School. Richman is president of Richman Associates, a bioscience communications company.

SOURCE: Nutan Sharma and Elaine Richman, *Parkinson's Disease and the Family: A New Guide.* Cambridge, MA: Harvard University Press, 2005. Copyright © 2005 by the President and Fellows of Harvard College. All rights reserved. Reproduced by permission of Harvard University Press.

Medical treatment refers primarily to the use of medicines to relieve symptoms. To date, there are no medications to stop the progression of Parkinson's disease. The majority of patients use a single medication or combination of medications to relieve their symptoms. There are a variety of medications available to treat the symptoms of Parkinson's disease.

The decision about when to start taking medication is individual and based on a patient's degree of disability and discomfort. Everyone's comfort level will be different, of course, so when prescribing medications, doctors consider not only symptoms, but also the individual's response to various dosages, and a host of social, occupational, and psychological issues.

From a doctor's perspective, the goal of pharmacological treatment is to help the patient function independently for as long as possible. Six classes of drugs are available to help accomplish that goal:

- anticholinergic agents
- antiviral drugs
- dopamine replacement agents
- dopamine agonists
- inhibitors of the enzyme monoamine oxidase B (MAO-B)
- inhibitors of the enzyme catechol-o-methyl transferase (COMT). . .

Anticholinergic agents. Anticholinergic agents are the oldest class of medications used for Parkinson's disease. They work by blocking the effects of a neurotransmitter [brain chemical] called acetylcholine and are most effective in reducing rest tremor and rigidity. However, they have side effects that typically limit their use. The side effects include dry mouth, constipation, urinary retention, blurred vision, confusion, and difficulty with concentration.

Antiviral agents. Amantadine (brand name Symmetrel) is also used to treat Parkinson's disease. Amantadine is classified as an antiviral drug. We do not fully understand how it works in Parkinson's disease. It is thought to work by augmenting the release of dopamine from those neurons that are viable and producing dopamine. Amantadine produces limited improvement in bradykinesia (slow movement), rigidity, and rest tremor. Amantadine is helpful in controlling dyskinesias [impaired ability to make the body move with intention] that can develop later in the course of Parkinson's disease. . . . Possible side effects include lower-extremity edema (swelling caused by accumulation of fluid), confusion, and hallucinations.

Dopamine replacement. Dopamine replacement is the cornerstone of therapy for Parkinson's disease. (Recall

Shown here are areas of the brain affected by Parkinson's, caused by a degeneration of nerve tissue in the basal ganglia of the brain. Normal nerve pathways (in black) contrast with dysfunctional pathways (in red). When dopamine (molecules at far left and right) cannot be produced, a loss of muscle control and tremors results. **(John Bavosi/Photo Researchers, Inc.)**

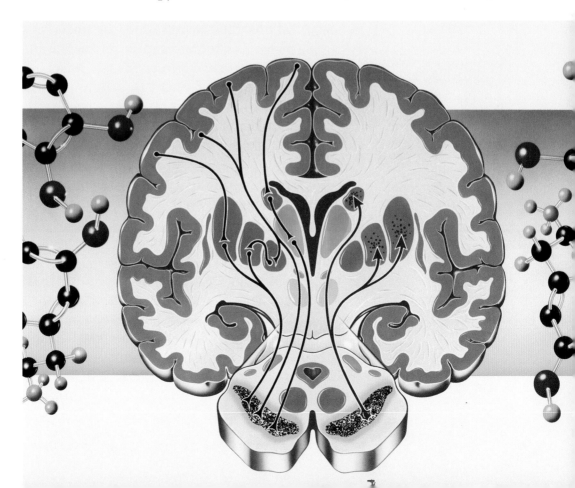

that Parkinson's disease results from the loss of brain cells that produce dopamine.) Patients actually take a drug called levodopa rather than dopamine. Levodopa is a natural precursor to dopamine and is given in combination with another medication called carbidopa. Carbidopa helps the levodopa enter the brain by blocking the breakdown of the drug in the bloodstream before it enters the brain itself.

Levodopa is most effective in reducing tremor, rigidity, and akinesia. The most common side effects, seen with the onset of treatment, are nausea and abdominal cramping. Long-term treatment with levodopa or the dopamine agonists is associated with two potential types of complications: hourly fluctuations in motor state and dyskinesias. It is not clear if these complications are due to the medications, the progression of the underlying disease, or some complex interaction between these two factors. . . .

FAST FACT

Alternative therapies for treating Parkinson's, including acupuncture, yoga, and massage, are often used in addition to medications.

Dopamine agonists. Dopamine agonists for Parkinson's disease work by directly stimulating dopamine receptors on brain cells. An agonist is a drug that binds to and activates a receptor on a cell, leading to changes within that cell. Dopamine agonists fool the brain into thinking that there is more dopamine present than is actually the case. There are several different dopamine agonists, and they can be used alone or in combination with levodopa therapy.

The older dopamine agonists, bromocriptine (Parlodel) and pergolide (Permax), are less specific in their actions than the newer agents. The newer dopamine agonists, pramipexole (Mirapex) and ropinerole (Requip), are thus, in theory, less likely to cause unpleasant side effects. However, the theoretical benefit to the newer dopamine agonists has not been conclusively demonstrated in long-term clinical trials. Compared with levodopa, both the new and the old dopamine agonists cause a lower occurrence of dyskinesias and a higher occurrence of confusion and hallucinations. To minimize the risk of intolerable side effects, patients should start with a small dose of medication and then slowly increase the total daily dosage.

MAO-B inhibitors of dopamine metabolism. Inhibitors of dopamine metabolism are also used to treat Parkinson's disease. Metabolism refers to the breakdown of a particular medication. Thus, agents that inhibit the metabolism of dopamine will allow the dopamine to remain in its active state for a longer period. Selegiline (Deprenyl) is an inhibitor of dopamine metabolism. It inhibits the enzyme monoamine oxidase B (MAO-B), which acts in the central nervous system by breaking down dopamine. Common side effects include dry mouth and dizziness.

COMT inhibitors of dopamine metabolism. Entacapone (Comtan) is another inhibitor of dopamine metabolism. Entacapone inhibits the activity of the enzyme called catechol-o-methyl transferase (COMT), which breaks down levodopa. Entacapone is taken in conjunction with a tablet of carbidopa/levodopa and acts to increase the amount of levodopa that reaches the brain. Common side effects include abdominal pain and fatigue. The benefits of entacapone treatment include a reduction in total daily levodopa dose and an improvement in the length of time of optimal mobility.

Recently a new combination pill of entacapone with carbidopa and levodopa has become available. The brand name of this drug is Stalevo. The advantage to this combination medication is that it reduces the number of tablets a person has to take on a daily basis. Common side effects of Stalevo include nausea and headache.

Tolcapone (Tasmar) is another inhibitor of catechol-o-methyl transferase. Like entacapone, tolcapone is taken in conjunction with a tablet of carbidopa/levodopa and acts to increase the amount of levodopa that reaches the

Medications Used in the Treatment of Parkinson's Disease

Drug class	Generic name	Brand name
Anticholinergic	Benztropine Trihexyphenidyl	Cogentin Artane
Antiviral	Amantadine	Symmetrel
Dopamine agonists	Bromocriptine Pergolide Ropinerole Pramipexole	Parlodel Permax Requip Mirapex
Dopamine replacement	Carbidopa/ levodopa	Sinemet
COMT inhibitor	Entacapone Tolcapone	Comtan Tasmar
MAO-B inhibitor	Selegiline	Deprenyl
Combination dopamine replacement + COMT inhibitor	Carbidopa/ levodopa + entacapone	Stalevo

Taken from: Nutan Sharma and Elaine Richman, *Parkinson's Disease and the Family.* Cambridge, MA: Harvard University Press, 2005.

brain. A rare but fatal risk from taking tolcapone is acute liver failure. Because of this risk, the use of tolcapone is typically limited to people who either cannot tolerate or do not derive benefits from other medications for their Parkinson's disease. . . .

Maintaining a Medication Schedule

There are several reasons for maintaining a daily schedule of medication doses. First, establishing a schedule makes it less likely that medications will be forgotten. Second, maintaining relatively steady levels of medication in the bloodstream (and, therefore, in the brain), allows a patient to control his or her symptoms to the greatest extent possible. Third, spacing out the medication doses at fairly regular intervals makes it less likely that side effects such as abdominal cramps or nausea will occur, these side effects are more common when there are excessively high levels of medication in the bloodstream.

Surgical Treatments
for Parkinson's

William J. Weiner, Lisa M. Shulman,
and Anthony E. Lang

Neurosurgery for Parkinson's disease is used to alleviate the symptoms and improve quality of life. In the following viewpoint William J. Weiner, Lisa M. Shulman, and Anthony E. Lang describe four different types of Parkinson's surgery. Two of these surgeries are currently in use; one involves creating permanent lesions on a specific area of the brain to help control tremors and rigidity, and the other uses surgically implanted electrodes to stimulate a specific area of the brain to relieve symptoms. Two other procedures are discussed that are currently being researched: nerve cell transplantation, which includes stem cells, and nerve growth factor injection. The authors state that neurosurgery may someday be used to apply gene therapy directly to the brain. Weiner is chairman of the Department of Neurology at the University of Maryland School of Medicine; Shulman is a professor of neurology at the University of Maryland School of

Medicine and codirector of the Maryland Parkinson's Disease and Movement Disorders Center; Lang is a professor at the University of Toronto and a specialist in movement disorders.

For decades, neurosurgeons have investigated the connection between the anatomy of the brain and the symptoms of Parkinson's disease. By interrupting various neural circuits within the brain, accomplished by carefully destroying a region of brain tissue in order to create a lesion, surgeons have sought to reduce a person's symptoms of tremor, rigidity, slowness, and postural problems. Neurosurgeons did not expect these procedures to cure or even delay progression of the disease, but they hoped to improve the symptoms and quality of life in people with advanced Parkinson's for whom medications were no longer as effective as they had been. . . .

Although creating a brain lesion may help alleviate the symptoms of Parkinson's, surgery does not cure or even slow the disease. Parkinson's remains a degenerative disease: it continues to get worse. Some neurosurgical centers report that some of the benefits of the surgery last for more than five years. Other centers report that some of the benefits begin to disappear after about a year. People with Parkinson's might ask, "If I have this surgery and it's useful to me for two years, is that worth it?" For some people, the answer is yes.

The History of Parkinson's Surgery

Surgical treatments for Parkinson's disease began in the 1930s, before the development of levodopa [a Parkinson's medication], and produced notably uneven results. Surgical lesions were mostly aimed at reducing tremor, but they also created new neurologic deficits such as paralysis and slurred speech. By the end of the 1960s, surgical strategies had evolved and neurosurgeons had learned which areas of the brain responded best to surgery and which surgical "targets" produced the fewest side effects.

Thereafter, surgery focused on two brain structures: the *thalamus* and the *globus pallidus*. The thalamus contains a number of distinct cell groups that are involved in complex relays—some of them from the globus pallidus—in the motor control circuits. . . . Physicians thought *thalamotomy* (the selective destruction of a small portion of the thalamus) and *pallidotomy* (the selective destruction of a small area of the globus pallidus) both offered potential relief from parkinsonian tremor and rigidity.

These neurosurgical procedures were in use in the 1950s and 1960s, before the levodopa era. Yet even then, the use of this "functional" neurosurgery (meaning surgery intended to improve *functioning*, not provide a cure) was not widespread. Such procedures provided benefits too inconsistently, and too frequently produced adverse effects. Surgery was used as a treatment for severe tremor, however, because very few useful medications were available.

Levodopa, highly effective in alleviating Parkinson's symptoms, emerged in the late 1960s, and many neurologists and neurosurgeons lost their enthusiasm for the surgical procedures with their attendant risks. The use of thalamotomy and pallidotomy virtually ceased, except in a few countries, including Sweden and Japan. Interest in thalamotomy has never been revived in the United States, because levodopa continues to be effective for treating the same symptoms relieved by this procedure and thalamotomy is effective only for tremor relief.

Pallidotomy has seen something of a resurgence in North America. The procedure resurfaced in the 1990s, in part because neurosurgeons have been able to make significant improvements in their techniques and now better understand the neural circuits that give rise to Parkinson's symptoms. In addition, drug-induced dyskinesia

—which in the 1960s, before levodopa was available, did not exist—is now a more common problem, one that responds well to surgical treatment. On the other hand, lesioning techniques, including pallidotomy, have been largely supplanted by the use of deep brain stimulation of various targets, particularly the subthalamic nucleus but also the globus pallidus and, to a lesser extent, the thalamus.

Four Surgical Procedures

Our discussion of neurosurgical approaches to Parkinson's disease focuses on four different procedures:

1. Thalamotomy and pallidotomy, the placement of lesions in the thalamus or globus pallidus

2. Deep brain stimulation of the thalamus, globus pallidus, or subthalamic nucleus

3. Nerve cell transplantation

4. Injection of nerve cell growth factors into the brain

The first two of these approaches are currently in use, whereas nerve cell transplantation and injection of nerve cell growth factors are available only through research programs that are investigating their safety and effectiveness. In the future, neurosurgery may be used to apply gene therapy to the brain. Genes or genetically manipulated cells could be introduced directly into the brain in the hope of repairing nerve cell damage, replacing the damaged cells, or providing nerve growth factors. . . .

Thalamotomy and Pallidotomy

Before performing thalamotomy or pallidotomy, surgeons and movement disorder specialists identify the target region of the brain by using one of several methods, including special computerized imaging systems, electrophysiologic recording from neurons in the brain, and special anatomic atlases. They also identify the nearby structures to avoid when creating the lesion.

During the surgery, a hole is made in the skull and thin probes with electrodes are passed through the hole to the target region. The patient is awake during the surgery. The patient does not experience pain but can have considerable discomfort associated with remaining on the operative table for a long period. During the procedure, the surgeon or the neurologist asks the patient to perform repetitive movements, such as opening and closing the hand and speaking, to confirm that the probe is located accurately in the target. Patients are frequently aware of the moment when their tremor or rigidity improves during the surgical procedure.

After the precise brain site has been identified, the surgeon gradually heats up the tip of the electrode until it irreversibly injures a small amount of brain tissue in the target area. In a thalamotomy, a small region in the thalamus is destroyed. This procedure is primarily useful for people with severe tremor; it may also relieve rigidity. Thalamotomy does little or nothing for other disabling features of Parkinson's such as slowness, clumsiness of movement, or walking difficulties and, as noted above, it is now seldom performed.

In a pallidotomy, a small region in the globus pallidus is destroyed. The current pallidotomy procedure creates a lesion in a slightly different area of the globus pallidus than did the older procedure. A lesion created in this new target area reliably affects Parkinson's symptoms. Many Parkinson's centers have now reported that this procedure is especially beneficial for drug-induced dyskinesia and can also relieve tremor, rigidity, and bradykinesia [slow movement]. . . .

In our view, pallidotomy should not be undertaken lightly. One reason is the continuing debate in the neurologic community about its proper role in treating Parkinson's disease. Some neurologists believe pallidotomy is appropriate mainly for people experiencing severe drug-induced dyskinesia. Other neurologists believe pallidotomy should be used for people with advanced Parkinson's who are having increasing difficulty with basic symptoms of the disease such as tremor, slowness, stiffness, and walking. However, the number of pallidotomies has decreased in recent years, because physicians' and patients' interest has shifted to the use of deep brain stimulation.

Another method of lesioning the thalamus or the pallidus without an open operation is the use of focused radiation with a *gamma knife.* Proponents of this technique argue that it is noninvasive and safer, especially for frail elderly patients or for patients in whom standard functional surgery is contraindicated (e.g., those with bleeding tendencies or who are taking anticoagulants). However, most functional neurosurgeons feel that this technique has problems, including the accuracy necessary to obtain optimal benefit, and side effects, due to the spread of the radiation-induced lesion beyond the desired area.

Deep Brain Stimulation

An important new surgical approach, deep brain stimulation (DBS) operates on a principle similar to pallidotomy or thalamotomy, except that in DBS a small area of the brain is *electrically stimulated* rather than destroyed. A neurosurgeon uses a probe to precisely place a small electrode at a specific location in the brain so as to interfere with the functioning of that area. Exactly how DBS works is not known. Initially, scientists believed that the electrical stimulation caused a temporary blockade of function in that area of the brain. We now know that the effects are probably more complex than this and could even vary depending on the site in the brain that is stimulated.

If DBS has an undesirable outcome, the stimulating electrodes can simply be turned off or the strength of the stimulus can be adjusted. This is very different from the situation with thalamotomy and pallidotomy, both of

Deep Brain Stimulation

This figure illustrates the placement of a deep-brain-stimulating electrode in the areas of the brain that are involved in motor dysfunction in Parkinson's disease. The procedure for deep brain stimulation involves placing an electrode deep within the brain, with the top portion situated just beneath the scalp and the lower portion attached to a stimulating box inserted beneath the skin of the chest wall (similar to the placement of a cardiac pacemaker). This figure shows only one side of the brain connected and stimulated. Most patients receiving subthalamic nucleus or globus pallidus stimulation undergo operations on both sides of the brain, with the two electrodes connected to a single pulse generator (stimulating box).

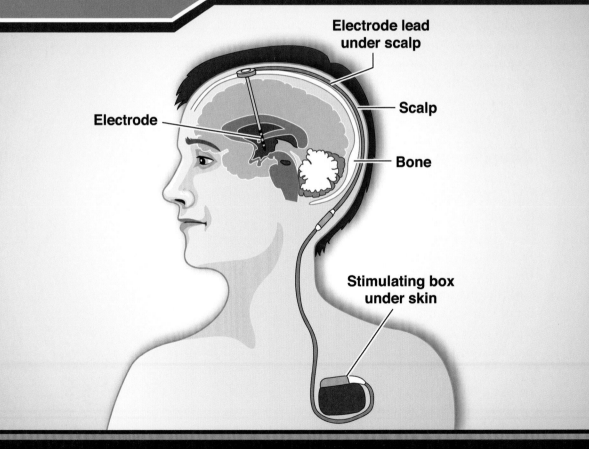

Electrode lead under scalp

Scalp

Electrode

Bone

Stimulating box under skin

Taken from: *Parkinson's Disease: A Complete Guide for Patients and Families.*
Baltimore: Johns Hopkins University Press, 2007.

which are irreversible. If a surgically created lesion leads to a bad outcome, such as a disturbance in the person's vision, there is no way to reverse the process. This is particularly risky in surgery performed on both sides of the brain, and these "bilateral" lesions result in a relatively high incidence of permanent complications, especially speech disturbances. Because of its reversibility, DBS should carry a lower risk, especially when applied to both sides of the brain.

In the DBS procedure, the Parkinson's team targets the area of the brain where they want to interfere with the functioning of brain circuits, make a hole in the skull, and insert the probe in a process very similar to thalamotomy and pallidotomy. Again, the patient is awake in order to provide feedback to the team for the electrode placement. When the team is satisfied with the placement, the final stimulating electrode is put in place.

A second procedure then follows, either immediately or up to a week later. With the patient under general anesthesia, the surgeon connects the electrode to a wire that runs under the skin to a stimulating box placed in a pouch under the skin on the chest wall. The box and the wire provide the electrical stimulus for the electrode. The arrangement is very similar to the placement of the power source of a cardiac pacemaker. Thus, in contrast to pallidotomy or thalamotomy, DBS requires two surgical procedures, one under general anesthetic.

Once the "pacemaker" is implanted, the patient can easily turn the stimulation on or off. When the stimulation is turned on, an electrical current passes from the electrode to the target region and temporarily disrupts the function of that area of the brain.

Deep brain stimulation has been approved for use in the United States for the treatment of Parkinson's. The target area can be the thalamus, globus pallidus, or subthalamic nucleus (STN). DBS of the thalamus is performed infrequently in Parkinson's since its effect is primarily limited to tremor reduction, whereas DBS of the globus pallidus and STN effectively relieves tremor as well as other disabling symptoms of Parkinson's disease. . . .

The only people for whom DBS placement for tremor should be considered are those with severe, incapacitating tremor that is unresponsive to medications. Those with mild or moderate tremor should not undergo the risk of DBS placement in the thalamus.

DBS Procedures Introduce Rewards and Risks

Recent years have seen a dramatic increase in the number of DBS procedures being performed for treatment of Parkinson's. . . .

Deep brain stimulation of the STN has proved very effective in alleviating not only tremors but rigidity and slowness. It is also effective in alleviating dyskinesia, although this effect is probably more related to most people being able to reduce their antiparkinson medications after DBS placement. Significantly, for many people who have DBS performed on both sides of the brain, "off" time is reduced and, on average, they have as much as six additional hours of "on" time. . . . This surgery is not appropriate for those who have substantial disability even in the best "on" state (e.g., slowness, walking problems, freezing, falling, severe speech problems). . . .

The surgical placement of the DBS electrode is accompanied by the same risks associated with other brain surgery: brain hemorrhage, stroke, partial loss of vision, infection, and paralysis. Because DBS requires the long-term placement of an electrode in the brain, connected by wires to a stimulator box in the upper chest, there are additional possibilities for complications, including infection at these remote sites or mechanical breakdowns that may require additional surgical corrections.

In the postoperative period, DBS requires repeated assessments to make sure the stimulation parameters and

antiparkinson drugs are optimal for the individual. These assessments can be time consuming and require considerable expertise to obtain the best clinical response with minimum side effects. In the initial days to weeks, patients may experience a variety of symptoms that could be the effects of excessive stimulation or stimulation at less than optimal sites, or of the need to adjust antiparkinson medications—either increase doses toward preoperative levels (if they have been reduced too quickly) or reduce doses, depending on the symptoms experienced. . . .

Doctors perform deep brain stimulation (DBS) on a patient afflicted with Parkinson's disease. DBS of the subthalamic nucleus has proved very effective in alleviating tremors, rigidity, and slowness. (AP Images)

Nerve Cell Transplantation

Another area of particular interest in surgical approaches to treating Parkinson's disease is nerve cell transplantation. The history of nerve cell transplantation began in the 1980s, when there was interest in transplanting *adrenal gland cells*, not nerve cells, into the brain of a person with Parkinson's. The tale of adrenal cell transplantation is a cautionary one. The principle behind the procedure was that cells could be taken from the adrenal gland in a patient's abdomen and inserted into her or his brain, where they would convert to dopamine-producing cells. At first the procedure was favorably reported in the medical literature, and the public media also covered the story. A considerable number of people underwent the transplantation, even though it was quite a major surgical procedure involving both abdominal surgery to remove the cells from the adrenal gland and neurosurgery to implant the cells into the brain. Subsequently, adrenal cell transplantation was found to be ineffective, and a review of the initial reports revealed that the early enthusiasm was based on highly suspect evidence. Adrenal cell transplantation into the brain has now been abandoned.

The principle behind transplanting nerve cells into the brain is similar. Currently interest is focused on *human fetal cell transplantation*. Human fetal cell transplantation is an experimental procedure. Nerve cells destined to become substantia nigra cells are taken from the brains of several aborted human fetuses in early development then implanted into the brain of the person with Parkinson's disease in the area where dopamine receptors are located. (The substantia nigra is the area that degenerates in Parkinson's.) The hope is that the human fetal cells will branch out, make contact with the dopamine receptors, and restore the motor control function.

Researchers in Sweden have been interested in this procedure for more than two decades. Over the last several years, Swedish centers have been following up on a small group of people who have undergone this procedure and have reported symptomatic improvement. Nonetheless, the Swedes concur that the procedure remains experimental. Several other countries, including Cuba and China, have centers where human fetal cell transplantation is available. Well-documented reports of patients who have undergone the transplantation procedures in these countries have not been presented in the scientific literature, so we can draw no conclusions.

Clinical Trials Raise Doubts

Despite the enormous favorable publicity about fetal cell transplantation for Parkinson's, two recent, well-conducted clinical trials sponsored by the National Institutes of Health have investigated whether or not fetal cell transplants actually have any benefit in Parkinson's. The first trial consisted of one group of Parkinson's patients receiving fetal cell implantations and a second group receiving "sham" surgery (surgery that "goes through the motions" but does not actually implant any cells; the sham surgery is thus a type of placebo). Sometime after the surgery, the investigators asked the study participants to answer questions about how well their symptoms were responding. Little difference in symptoms was reported by the two groups and, in people over the age of sixty, no difference was reported at all. The second trial compared a sham surgery group with groups that received transplanted cells from one to four fetuses per side of the brain. Once again, this study failed to show benefit from the fetal transplantation. Importantly, some of the patients in both of these studies developed disabling dyskinesia as a complication of the transplantation, which unlike drug-related dyskinesia, has persisted despite withdrawal of dopaminergic drugs. The development of so-called runaway dyskinesia has markedly slowed clinical trials exploring this idea. It is generally agreed in the research community that large trials should be stopped until this unusual adverse event is better understood. This is particularly important because no motor benefit was observed. Even if these trials had been successful, it seems unlikely that this therapy will become widely used. The procedure requires an extensive team of investigators to harvest the fetal cells, test the cells for infection, store the cells, dissect the cells, and finally, transplant them into the patient's brain. This procedure involves enormous time and effort, requires a large number of fetuses (up to eight per patient), and poses a number of serious ethical issues. . . .

Nerve Growth Factors

Another therapy under study is the use of nerve growth factors, which may provide new approaches to treatment. Nerve growth factors (also called *neurotrophic factors*) are chemical substances within the brain that facilitate the survival and development of nerve cells. We have discussed in earlier [work] how nerve cells use chemicals called neurotransmitters (such as dopamine) to communicate with one another. Neurotrophic factors are additional chemicals within the brain that are critical for nerve cell survival.

Of the several different types of neurotrophic factors identified, *glial-derived neurotrophic factor* (GDNF) is one of the most important to the survival and growth of dopamine-producing cells. Some researchers suggest that GDNF can improve survival of the dopamine-producing nerve cells in people with Parkinson's, improve their symptoms, and perhaps even slow down the progress of Parkinson's. GDNF has been shown to work well in monkeys. Unfortunately, this is another example of a potential therapy that seems to work very well in animals but not in people with Parkinson's.

GDNF is a very large molecule and cannot cross the blood-brain barrier, so it cannot be taken by mouth or by the usual injection techniques. Delivery of GDNF to the brain requires surgery. There have been two different approaches to delivery of GDNF to the brain of people with Parkinson's. In the first trial of GDNF, the chemical was delivered into the ventricles (the large fluid-filled spaces in every brain) via a special catheter (very narrow tube) passing through a small hole in the skull. This trial failed, and many researchers believed that GDNF failed to improve Parkinson's symptoms because it entered the fluid-filled space and never really got to the site in the brain where it was needed. A second trial of GDNF delivered the chemical directly into brain tissue ("intraparenchymal" injection) in the region most affected by dopamine deficiency in Parkinson's (the putamen) via another type of catheter. This trial was stopped for several reasons: there was no statistically significant beneficial effect, some patients developed antibodies to GDNF, and some reports suggested that GDNF might produce abnormalities in the brain of certain animals.

There was considerable publicity associated with the decision to stop the trial, because some people who had received the drug felt they had benefited. But overall, there was no evidence that intraparenchymal injection of GDNF helped in Parkinson's disease. . . .

GDNF remains a very interesting substance that may yet find a role in the therapy of Parkinson's. Researchers who have treated a small number of patients with different doses of GDNF, and using different types of catheters than were used in the placebo-controlled trial described above, continue to argue that their patients have benefited from the treatment. Some researchers are now working on delivering genes into the brain that will produce excess GDNF or related growth factors as a way of treating Parkinson's.

The Future of Parkinson's Disease

National Institute of Neurological Disorders and Stroke

In the following viewpoint, the National Institute of Neurological Disorders and Stroke discusses new treatments being developed for Parkinson's disease. According to the National Institutes of Health, the goals of halting the progression of the disease and restoring lost motor functions are realistic. One of the most promising avenues of research is genetics. Researchers have identified genes that are linked to individuals with Parkinson's and genes that may play a role in causing the disease. Another avenue of study is focusing on biomarkers—certain body characteristics that tell if the disease is progressing. These markers can help diagnose the disease before symptoms appear and help determine how well treatments are working. Cell therapies, including stem cell research, are also a large part of continuing Parkinson's studies. The National Institute of Neurological Disorders and Stroke is part of the National Institutes of Health and focuses on disease-related research in neuroscience.

SOURCE: National Institute of Neurological Disorders and Stroke, *Parkinson's Disease: Hope Through Research*, NIH Publication No. 06–139. Bethesda, MD: National Institute of Neurological Disorders and Stroke, National Institutes of Health, 2008.

In recent years, Parkinson's research has advanced to the point that halting the progression of PD [Parkinson's disease], restoring lost function, and even preventing the disease are all considered realistic goals. While the ultimate goal of preventing PD may take years to achieve, researchers are making great progress in understanding and treating PD.

Genetic Research May Prove Useful

One of the most exciting areas of PD research is genetics. Studying the genes responsible for inherited cases can help researchers understand both inherited and sporadic cases of the disease. Identifying gene defects can also help researchers understand how PD occurs, develop animal models that accurately mimic the neuronal death in human PD, identify new drug targets, and improve diagnosis. . . .

Several genes have been definitively linked to PD in some people. Researchers also have identified a number of other genes that may play a role and are working to confirm these findings. In addition, several chromosomal regions have been linked to PD in some families. Researchers hope to identify the genes located in these chromosomal regions and to determine which of them may play roles in PD.

Researchers funded by NINDS [National Institute of Neurological Disorders and Stroke] are gathering information and DNA samples from hundreds of families with PD and are conducting large-scale gene expression studies to identify genes that are abnormally active or inactive in PD. They also are comparing gene activity in PD with gene activity in similar diseases such as progressive supranuclear palsy.

Some scientists have found evidence that specific variations in the DNA of mitochondria—structures in cells that provide the energy for cellular activity—can increase the risk of getting PD, while other variations are

Experimental Gene Therapy

Preliminary evidence suggests that an experimental gene therapy procedure could ease Parkinson's symptoms with no side effects.

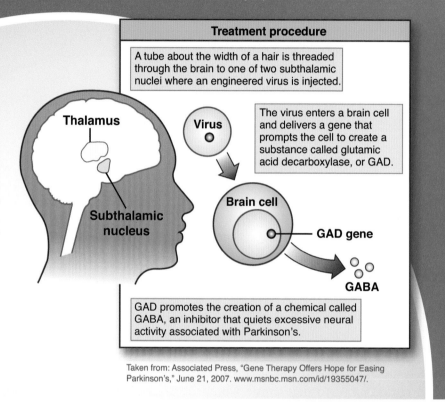

Treatment procedure

A tube about the width of a hair is threaded through the brain to one of two subthalamic nuclei where an engineered virus is injected.

Thalamus

Virus

The virus enters a brain cell and delivers a gene that prompts the cell to create a substance called glutamic acid decarboxylase, or GAD.

Brain cell

Subthalamic nucleus

GAD gene

GABA

GAD promotes the creation of a chemical called GABA, an inhibitor that quiets excessive neural activity associated with Parkinson's.

Taken from: Associated Press, "Gene Therapy Offers Hope for Easing Parkinson's," June 21, 2007. www.msnbc.msn.com/id/19355047/.

associated with a lowered risk of the disorder. They also have found that PD patients have more mitochondrial DNA (mtDNA) variations than patients with other movement disorders or Alzheimer's disease. Researchers are working to define how these mtDNA variations may lead to PD.

In addition to identifying new genes for PD, researchers are trying to learn how known PD genes function and how the gene mutations cause disease. For example, a 2005 study found that the normal alpha-synuclein protein may help other proteins that are important for nerve transmission to fold correctly. Other studies have suggested that the normal parkin protein protects neurons from a variety of threats, including alpha-synuclein toxicity and excitotoxicity.

Other Areas of Research

Scientists continue to study environmental toxins such as pesticides and herbicides that can cause PD symptoms in animals. They have found that exposing rodents to the pesticide rotenone and several other agricultural chemicals can cause cellular and behavioral changes that mimic those seen in PD. Other studies have suggested that prenatal exposure to certain toxins can increase susceptibility to PD in adulthood. An NIH [National Institutes of Health]-sponsored program called the Collaborative Centers for Parkinson's Disease Environmental Research (CCPDER) focuses on how occupational exposure to toxins and use of caffeine and other substances may affect the risk of PD.

Another major area of PD research involves the cell's protein disposal system, called the ubiquitin-proteasome system. If this disposal system fails to work correctly, toxins and other substances may build up to harmful levels, leading to cell death. The ubiquitin-proteasome system requires interactions between several proteins, including parkin and UCH-L1. Therefore, disruption of the ubiquitin-proteasome system may partially explain how mutations in these genes cause PD.

Other studies focus on how Lewy bodies [abnormal accumulation of protein within nerve cells] form and what role they play in PD. Some studies suggest that Lewy bodies are a byproduct of degenerative processes within neurons, while others indicate that Lewy bodies are a protective mechanism by which neurons lock away abnormal molecules that might otherwise be harmful. Additional studies have found that alpha-synuclein clumps alter gene expression and bind to vesicles within the cell in ways that could be harmful.

Another common topic of PD research is excitotoxicity —overstimulation of nerve cells that leads to cell damage or death. In excitotoxicity, the brain becomes oversensitized to the neurotransmitter glutamate, which increases activity in the brain. The dopamine deficiency in PD causes overactivity of neurons in the subthalamic nucleus, which may lead to excitotoxic damage there and in other parts of the brain. Researchers also have found that dysfunction of the cells' mitochondria can make dopamine-producing neurons vulnerable to glutamate.

Inflammation and Biomarker Research

Other researchers are focusing on how inflammation may affect PD. Inflammation is common to a variety of neurodegenerative diseases, including PD, Alzheimer's disease, HIV-1-associated dementia, and amyotrophic lateral sclerosis. Several studies have shown that inflammation-promoting molecules increase cell death after treatment with the toxin MPTP. Inhibiting the inflammation with drugs or by genetic engineering prevented some of the neuronal degeneration in these studies. Other research has shown that dopamine neurons in brains from patients with PD have higher levels of an inflammatory enzyme called COX-2 than those of people without PD. Inhibiting COX-2 doubled the number of neurons that survived in a mouse model for PD.

Since the discovery that MPTP causes parkinsonian symptoms in humans, scientists have found that by injecting MPTP and certain other toxins into laboratory animals, they can reproduce the brain lesions that cause these symptoms. This allows them to study the mechanisms of the disease and helps in the development of new treatments. They also have developed animal models with alterations of the alpha-synuclein and parkin genes. Other researchers have used genetic engineering to develop mice with disrupted mitochondrial function in dopamine neurons. These animals have many of the characteristics associated with PD.

Biomarkers for PD—measurable characteristics that can reveal whether the disease is developing or progressing—are another focus of research. Such biomarkers could help doctors detect the disease before symptoms appear and improve diagnosis of the disease. They also would show if medications and other types of therapy have a positive or negative effect on the course of the disease. Some of the most promising biomarkers for PD are brain imaging techniques. For example, some researchers are using positron-emission tomography (PET) brain scans to try to identify metabolic changes in the brains of people with PD and to determine how these changes relate to disease symptoms. Other potential biomarkers for PD include alterations in gene expression.

Researchers also are conducting many studies of new or improved therapies for PD. While deep brain stimulation (DBS) is now FDA [Food and Drug Administration]-approved and has been used in thousands of people with PD, researchers continue to try to improve the technology and surgical techniques in this therapy. For example, some studies are comparing DBS to the best medical therapy and trying to determine which part of the brain is the best location for stimulation. Another clinical trial is studying how DBS affects depression and quality of life.

Other clinical studies are testing whether transcranial electrical polarization (TEP) or transcranial magnetic stimulation (TMS) can reduce the symptoms of PD. In TEP, electrodes placed on the scalp are used to generate an electrical current that modifies signals in the brain's cortex. In TMS, an insulated coil of wire on the scalp is used to generate a brief electrical current.

Drug Research

One of the enduring questions in PD research has been how treatment with levodopa and other dopaminergic

FAST FACT

The average age of onset of Parkinson's disease is sixty; 60 percent of patients are at least this age when diagnosed.

drugs affects progression of the disease. Researchers are continuing to try to clarify these effects. One study has suggested that PD patients with a low-activity variant of the gene for COMT (which breaks down dopamine) perform worse than others on tests of cognition [brain function], and that dopaminergic drugs may worsen cognition in these people, perhaps because the reduced COMT activity causes dopamine to build up to harmful levels in some parts of the brain. In the future, it may become possible to test for such individual gene differences in order to improve treatment of PD.

A variety of new drug treatments are in clinical trials for PD. These include a drug called GM1 ganglioside that increases dopamine levels in the brain. Researchers are testing whether this drug can reduce symptoms, delay disease progression, or partially restore damaged brain cells in PD patients. Other studies are testing whether a drug called istradefylline can improve motor function in PD, and whether a drug called ACP-103 that blocks receptors for the neurotransmitter serotonin will lessen the severity of parkinsonian symptoms and levodopa-associated complications in PD patients. Other topics of research include controlled-release formulas of PD drugs and implantable pumps that give a continuous supply of levodopa.

Some researchers are testing potential neuroprotective drugs to see if they can slow the progression of PD. One study, called NET-PD (Neuroexploratory Trials in Parkinson's Disease), is evaluating minocycline, creatine, coenzyme Q10, and GP1-1485 to determine if any of these agents should be considered for further testing. The NET-PD study may evaluate other possible neuroprotective agents in the future. Drugs found to be successful in the pilot phases may move to large phase III trials involving hundreds of patients. A separate group of researchers is investigating the effects of either 1200 or 2400 milligrams of coenzyme Q10 in 600 patients. Several MAO-B inhibitors, including selegiline, lazabemide, and rasagiline, also are in clinical trials to determine if they have neuroprotective effects in people with PD.

Nerve growth factors, or neurotrophic factors, which support survival, growth, and development of brain cells, are another type of potential therapy for PD. One such drug, glial cell line–derived neurotrophic factor (GDNF), has been shown to protect dopamine neurons and to promote their survival in animal models of PD. This drug has been tested in several clinical trials for people with PD, and the drug appeared to cause regrowth of dopamine nerve fibers in one person who received the drug. However, a phase II clinical study of GDNF was halted in 2004 because the treatment did not show any clinical benefit after 6 months, and some data suggested that it might even be harmful. Other neurotrophins that may be useful for treating PD include neurotrophin-4 (NT-4), brain-derived neurotrophic factor (BDNF), and fibroblast growth factor 2 (FGF-2).

A Wide Range of Treatments Are Explored

While there is currently no proof that any dietary supplements can slow PD, several clinical studies are testing whether supplementation with vitamin B12 and other substances may be helpful. A 2005 study found that dietary restriction—reducing the number of calories normally consumed—helped to increase abnormally low levels of the neurotransmitter glutamate in a mouse model for early PD. The study also suggested that dietary restriction affected dopamine activity in the brain. Another study showed that dietary restriction before the onset of PD in a mouse model helped to protect dopamine-producing neurons.

Other studies are looking at treatments that might improve some of the secondary symptoms of PD, such as depression and swallowing disorders. One clinical trial is investigating whether a drug called quetiapine can reduce psychosis or agitation in PD patients with dementia and in dementia patients with parkinsonian symptoms. Some studies also are examining whether transcranial magnetic stimulation or a food supplement called s-adenosyl-methionine (SAM-e) can alleviate depression in people with PD, and whether levetiracetam, a drug approved to

A technician extracts from a freezer a container of stem cells for use in developing cell therapies for Parkinson's disease sufferers. (Javier Soriano/AFP/Getty Images)

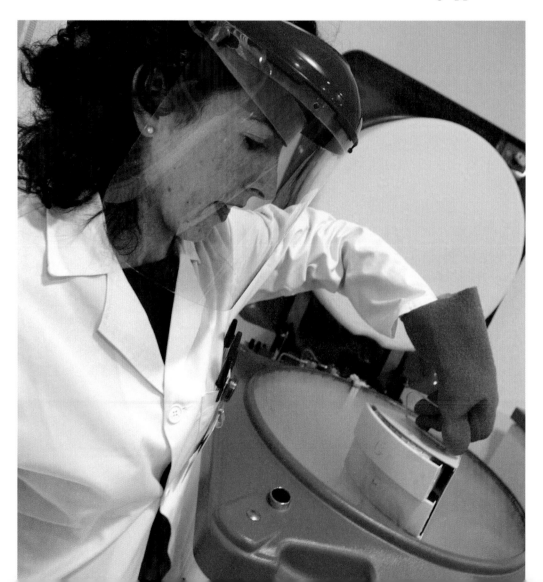

treat epilepsy, can reduce dyskinesias in Parkinson's patients without interfering with other PD drugs.

Another approach to treating PD is to implant cells to replace those lost in the disease. Researchers are conducting clinical trials of a cell therapy in which human retinal epithelial cells attached to microscopic gelatin beads are implanted into the brains of people with advanced PD. The retinal epithelial cells produce levodopa. The investigators hope that this therapy will enhance brain levels of dopamine.

Cell and Gene Therapies

Starting in the 1990s, researchers conducted a controlled clinical trial of fetal tissue implants in people with PD. They attempted to replace lost dopamine-producing neurons with healthy ones from fetal tissue in order to improve movement and the response to medications. While many of the implanted cells survived in the brain and produced dopamine, this therapy was associated with only modest functional improvements, mostly in patients under the age of 60. Unfortunately, some of the people who received the transplants developed disabling dyskinesias that could not be relieved by reducing antiparkinsonian medications.

Another type of cell therapy involves stem cells. Stem cells derived from embryos can develop into any kind of cell in the body, while others, called progenitor cells, are more restricted. One study transplanted neural progenitor cells derived from human embryonic stem cells into a rat model of PD. The cells appeared to trigger improvement on several behavioral tests, although relatively few of the transplanted cells became dopamine-producing neurons. Other researchers are developing methods to improve the number of dopamine-producing cells that can be grown from embryonic stem cells in culture.

Researchers also are exploring whether stem cells from adult brains might be useful in treating PD. They

Stem Cell Transplants Can Aid in Dopamine Production

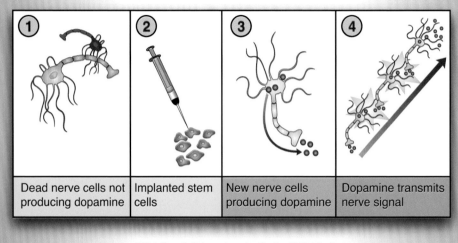

1	2	3	4
Dead nerve cells not producing dopamine	Implanted stem cells	New nerve cells producing dopamine	Dopamine transmits nerve signal

Taken from: University of Utah Genetic Science Learning Center, 2008. http://learn.genetics.utah.edu.

have shown that the brain's white matter contains multipotent progenitor cells that can multiply and form all the major cell types of the brain, including neurons.

Gene therapy is yet another approach to treating PD. A study of gene therapy in non-human primate models of PD is testing different genes and gene-delivery techniques in an effort to refine this kind of treatment. An early-phase clinical study is also testing whether using the adeno-associated virus type 2 (AAV2) to deliver the gene for a nerve growth factor called neurturin is safe for use in people with PD. Another study is testing the safety of gene therapy using AAV to deliver a gene for human aromatic L-amino acid decarboxylase, an enzyme that helps convert levodopa to dopamine in the brain. Other investigators are testing whether gene therapy to increase the amount of glutamic acid decarboxylase, which helps produce an inhibitory neurotransmitter called GABA, might reduce the overactivity of neurons in the brain that results from lack of dopamine.

Another potential approach to treating PD is to use a vaccine to modify the immune system in a way that can protect dopamine-producing neurons. One vaccine study in mice used a drug called copolymer-1 that increases the number of immune T cells that secrete anti-inflammatory cytokines and growth factors. The researchers injected copolymer-1-treated immune cells into a mouse model for PD. The vaccine modified the behavior of supporting (glial) cells in the brain so that their responses were beneficial rather than harmful. It also reduced the amount of neurodegeneration in the mice, reduced inflammation, and increased production of nerve growth factors. Another study delivered a vaccine containing alpha-synuclein in a mouse model of PD and showed that the mice developed antibodies that reduced the accumulation of abnormal alpha-synuclein. While these studies are preliminary, investigators hope that similar approaches might one day be tested in humans.

GDNF Is Beneficial to Parkinson's Patients

Linda Herman

In 2004 Amgen Inc., a biotechnology company, stopped trials of the Parkinson's disease drug GDNF (glial cell line–derived neurotrophic factor), and many people are still questioning that decision. In the following viewpoint Linda Herman discusses the fact that many individuals taking part in the study saw dramatic improvements in their disease symptoms. She also discusses and refutes Amgen's claims that the drug was unsafe for humans. Linda Herman is an author and a Parkinson's disease advocate.

[D]uring 2005 and 2006,] since Amgen halted its phase II trial of infusion delivery of GDNF [glial cell line–derived neurotrophic factor], there has been no scientific evidence released that proves any harm to humans from this drug. The question is— just how much harm is going to come from GDNF being

Photo on facing page. A research technician slices one half of a human brain into sections. The brain sections will be used to research neurodegenerative disorders, such as Parkinson's disease. (James King-Holmes/ Photo Researchers, Inc.)

withheld? When compared to risks of living with Parkinson's, trial participants say "a lot."

Many of us have met Steve Kaufman and seen the benefits he realized from GDNF with our own eyes. We have read about Richard Hembrough in the UK [United Kingdom] who after 31 years with PD [Parkinson's disease] and 2 1/2 years of GDNF treatment, no longer requires levodopa. We've listened to Robert Suthers on *60 Minutes* describe his improvements and subsequent decline after the trial halt. Statistics cannot obscure what these patients have experienced. They know and we know these were not placebo effects.

When Amgen initially halted the GDNF trial they cited three reasons:

1. The study failed to meet its clinical endpoint, which was a 25% improvement in UPDRS [Unified Parkinson's Disease Rating Scale] scores after 6 months.

2. Some patients developed antibodies to GDNF.

3. Four trial monkeys developed cerebellar lesions.

All of these issues—the trial design, the statistics, and the safety issues—have since been challenged in peer-reviewed journals.

Safety Issues Do Not Hold Up

The safety issues have been much publicized by Amgen's press releases.

Brain lesions found in monkey brains of experimental primates were the initial cause to halt the trial in August 2004. On the request of several study doctors FDA [Food and Drug Administration] reviewed these findings in January, 2005. Reports from that meeting indicate that FDA agreed to allow the existing GDNF participants to continue in the study, and recommended additional analyses before proceeding with new subjects. But Amgen has not released these data. Requests for release of their monkey toxicology data

In 2004, when biotechnology company Amgen, Inc. stopped trials of the Parkinson's drug GDNF due to possible health risks to patients, experts in the scientific community challenged the company's decision. **(AP Images)**

has yielded nothing. Amgen claims they are preparing it for publication. . . .

In the May 2006 issue of *Neurosurgical Focus,* however, researchers at the University of Kentucky confirmed that there has been no brain damage or long term side effects among their trial patients, and that they believe the research should continue. [According to John Slevin], "Unilateral administration of GDNF results in significant, sustained bilateral benefits. . . . Safety concerns with GDNF therapy can be closely monitored and managed."

Related investigations also reported in the April 2006 issue of *Experimental Neurology,* that they found "no imaging evidence of cerebellar injury in human subjects undergoing intracerebral GDNF infusion [according to Himachandra Chebrolu]."

Indeed, [Richard Penn reports in the *Lancet Neurology*] "no clinically significant adverse effects were ever seen in patients from either phase, some of whom took GDNF for 3 years."

Antibody Issues Raise Questions

The other key safety issue regarding development of antibodies by several participants was known at the time the initial results were released. Although this was a concern, no harmful effects from this condition were seen for GDNF or for other treatments where it has occurred. These antibodies may have occurred only in patients whose catheters became dislodged during the course of treatment—a problem that could be easily remedied. Some researchers believe these patients were not getting the GDNF into the brain; instead it may have been pumped into other parts of the body. These findings have not been made available to the public by Amgen.

The statistical analysis and conclusions of the Amgen phase II study have now also been challenged in the current issue [Summer 2006] of the *Journal of Neuroscience Methods.* "The study was found to be underpowered and thus incapable of ruling out a large effect of GDNF on Parkinson disease. It therefore does not contradict the large effects seen in previous open-label studies."

In the [2006 Anthony E.] Lang article itself [in the *Annals of Neurology*] inconsistencies were noted between the Phase I trials and the Amgen trial—different GDNF dosages, catheters (diameter size, number of ports), and

> **FAST FACT**
>
> The protein GDNF is produced in the central nervous system.

infusion methods (constant versus pulsed), which may have accounted for differing outcomes.

Research Should Continue

Given the overwhelmingly positive phase I trial results, and the inconclusive results of the phase II trial, the research should have been continued.

Infusion delivery of GDNF is our "bird-in-the-hand." No other neurorestorative and neuroprotective treatments are so far along in development at this time. The trial participants and every PD patient has been denied a likely effective treatment, that could have been available in the near future—much sooner than the "5–10 years" often predicted for unproven delivery methods of GDNF, such as gene therapy.

GDNF Is Harmful to Parkinson's Patients

Amgen Inc.

In the fall of 2004, Amgen Inc. halted a phase II trial of the Parkinson's drug GDNF (glial cell line–derived neurotrophic factor) citing no significant patient improvement with the drug. According to an earlier press release, patients "showed no clinical improvement compared to placebo following six months of treatment." In the following viewpoint Amgen explains that further analysis of the initial study data revealed that continued use of GDNF could have permanently harmful effects on patients. The company explains that the health risks to the study participants were too high to continue with the trial. Amgen Inc. is a biotechnology company that specializes in medical products and medications.

Citing patient safety concerns and scientific findings, Amgen Inc. announced today [February 11, 2005] that it has confirmed its previous decision

Citing safety concerns, Roger M. Perlmutter, head of research and development at Amgen, speaks to the press about the company's decision to discontinue the Parkinson's drug GDNF. **(Ken Cedeno/ Bloomberg News/Landov)**

to halt clinical trials of the experimental drug GDNF (Glial cell line–derived neurotrophic factor). Amgen halted studies of GDNF when scientific results indicated that allowing patients to continue treatment could potentially cause permanent harm, complicating an already devastating disease.

As part of that decision, and based on thorough scientific review, Amgen has also concluded that it will not provide GDNF to the 48 patients who participated in clinical trials that were terminated in the fall of 2004.

The Amgen Perspective

"We've looked at this decision from every perspective—scientific, medical and ethical. Our hearts truly go out to trial patients and their families, but we simply cannot allow trials to continue given the potential safety risks and the absence of proven benefit. Encouraging patients to continue in the GDNF study deters them from pursuing potentially helpful Parkinson's disease therapies that are already approved and available," said Kevin Sharer, Amgen's chairman and chief executive officer. "Our desire is to actively pursue GDNF in a meaningful way that may benefit all Parkinson's disease patients."

"We are deeply disappointed in the outcome of the trial and have enormous respect for the trial patients who struggle courageously to deal with the terrible effects of the disease," stated Roger M. Perlmutter, executive vice president, Research and Development, Amgen. "After careful review, we stand behind our decision to stop providing GDNF to patients due to potential safety risks observed in preclinical studies, including irreversible brain damage, and the absence of any demonstrated medical benefit. We adhered to the same high standards of practice we apply to all our clinical trials in making this decision."

> **FAST FACT**
>
> One of the major functions of the protein gene GDNF is to support the survival of dopaminergic neurons that die with Parkinson's disease.

"A team of Amgen researchers, clinicians and executives spent several months reviewing the company's initial decision to halt GDNF clinical trials. After exhaustive deliberation and input from trial investigators, patients, the FDA [Food and Drug Administration] and consulting experts and ethicists we confirmed our decision to halt the GDNF study," added Sharer.

Amgen's History with Parkinson's

Amgen has actively studied Parkinson's disease therapies for more than a decade and will continue to support GDNF and the Parkinson's disease community by continuing to conduct additional research to better under-

Neuronal Pathways That Degenerate in Parkinson's Disease

Movement signals travel from the substantia nigra to the striatum. In Parkinson's patients, the neurons carrying these signals degenerate.

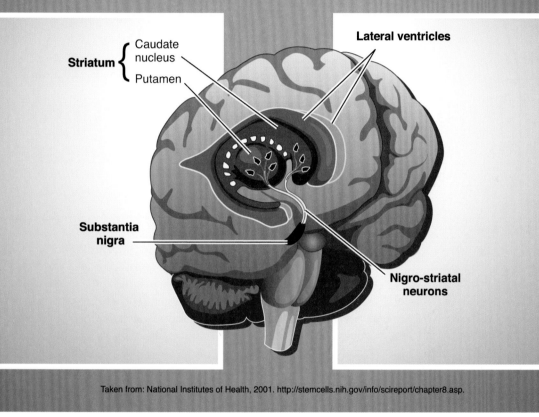

Striatum { Caudate nucleus / Putamen

Lateral ventricles

Substantia nigra

Nigro-striatal neurons

Taken from: National Institutes of Health, 2001. http://stemcells.nih.gov/info/scireport/chapter8.asp.

stand the potential of GDNF in the treatment of this terrible disease.

Discussions have been initiated with patient advocacy groups and research funding agencies to make Amgen's GDNF and other proprietary GDNF-related materials available to qualified pre-clinical researchers. Additionally, Amgen will pursue publication of both the Phase 2 study and toxicology data to further scientific understanding. Amgen will also expand the toxicology studies and work on discoveries to improve delivery of the drug.

A Low-Calorie Diet May Help in the Treatment of Parkinson's Disease

Oregon Health & Science University

In the following viewpoint Oregon Health & Science University discusses a new study that shows that a lower-calorie diet may help increase brain chemical levels in Parkinson's patients. According to the study, certain markers in the brain are showing that restricting diet may be helpful in readjusting levels of glutamate, a brain chemical involved in motor control. Some results show that getting glutamate levels back to normal may influence the reversal of some Parkinson's symptoms. Oregon Health & Science University is a health and research institution in Portland.

A new Oregon Health & Science University [OHSU] and Portland Veterans Affairs Medical Center [VAMC] study suggests that early-stage Parkinson's disease patients who lower their calorie intake may

SOURCE: Oregon Health & Science University, "Restricting Diet May Reverse Early-Stage Parkinson's," ohsu.edu, November 14, 2005. Copyright © 2001–2008, Oregon Health & Science University. Reproduced by permission.

boost levels of an essential brain chemical lost from the neurodegenerative disorder.

The study by Charles Meshul, Ph.D., associate professor of behavioral neuroscience in the OHSU School of Medicine and the VAMC's Neurocytology Lab, shows that dietary restriction reverses a Parkinson's-induced drop in glutamate, a brain neurotransmitter important for motor control, function and learning, in a mouse model for the disease's early stages.

The results, presented today [November 14, 2005] at the Society for Neuroscience's 35th annual meeting in Washington, D.C., are the first to show that a restricted diet can disable neurochemical changes in the brain occurring in early-stage Parkinson's even after those changes are observed.

"In the early stages of the disease, we see certain markers in the brain that are changing that may be indicative that dietary restriction is helpful," Meshul said.

The Influence and Prevalence of Parkinson's

Parkinson's disease is a progressive, degenerative disorder affecting a region of the brain called the substantia nigra where movement is controlled. Symptoms such as tremor or shaking, muscular stiffness or rigidity, slowness of movement and difficulty with balance appear when about 80 percent of cells in the body that produce the neurochemical dopamine die or become impaired.

> **FAST FACT**
>
> Protein-rich diets may contribute to the "on and off" cycles experienced by Parkinson's patients.

Incidence increases with age, and the disease is uncommon in people younger than 40. According to the OHSU Parkinson Center of Oregon, the disease affects both men and women across all ethnic lines and occurs in about two of every 100 people older than 55. About 1.5 million Americans suffer from the disease.

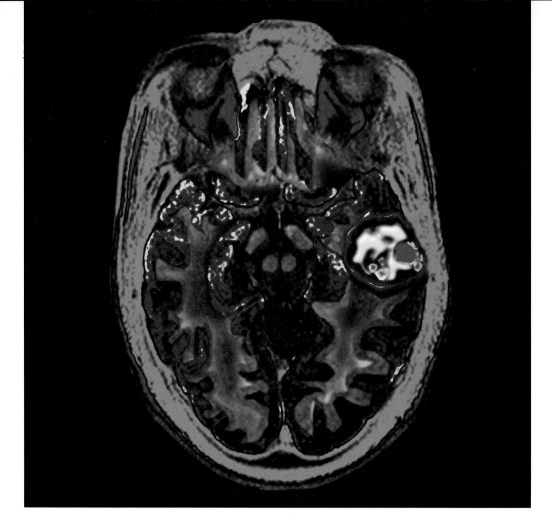

In this color magnetic resonance image of the brain, the substantia nigra is shown in bands of purple. The substantia nigra is where movement is controlled and is the area of the brain most affected by Parkinson's disease. (Living Art Enterprises, LLC/Photo Researchers, Inc.)

Meshul's lab compared two groups of mice with 60 percent to 75 percent loss of dopamine in the brain, representing early-stage Parkinson's: One had access to food every day while the other had access every other day, and both were fed over a 21-day period. The mice that ate less often lost 10 percent to 15 percent of their body weight compared to their counterparts.

"Dietary restriction appears to be normalizing the levels of glutamate," Meshul said. "The fact that we're getting the levels of glutamate back to, essentially, control levels may indicate there are certain synapse changes going on in the brain to counteract the effects of Parkinson's. In fact, what this may indicate is a reversal of locomotor deficits associated with the disease."

Dietary Restriction Delivers Real Chemical Results

In addition to the rise in glutamate, Meshul's group, using a dopamine-synthesizing enzyme called tyrosine hydroxylase as a marker for dopamine nerve terminals, found that dietary restriction caused a drop in the number of dopamine terminals in the mouse model for early-stage Parkinson's.

"As it turns out, dietary restriction, in and of itself, had an effect. It actually caused a small but significant decrease in the numbers of these dopamine terminals. So in other words, dietary restriction really is doing something to the brain," Meshul said. "It could very well be that what dietary restriction is doing is trying to protect the system somehow. And one of the reasons dietary restriction is protective may be that it's reducing the activity of particular synapses. That's actually what the data indicates."

Matching the upturn in glutamate levels with positive behavioral changes is difficult at this point in the research, Meshul said. "One of the unfortunate problems with this model is it's tough to do any behavioral measures. We see a reversal of the effect of glutamate in the brain due to the dietary restriction, but what does that actually mean in terms of the behavior of the animal? Unfortunately, we don't know. We didn't measure that."

But a similar primate study at the University of Southern California that Meshul is associated with is testing the hypothesis that glutamate does have an effect on behavior. "It turns out that, in time, these animals recover behaviorally from all of the motor deficits that are associated with (early-stage Parkinson's)," he said. "Our hypothesis is there may be changes in glutamate that account for these behavioral changes."

Diet Restriction Has Far-Reaching Benefits

Dietary restriction's beneficial effect on neurological function has been studied in primates by scientists at the

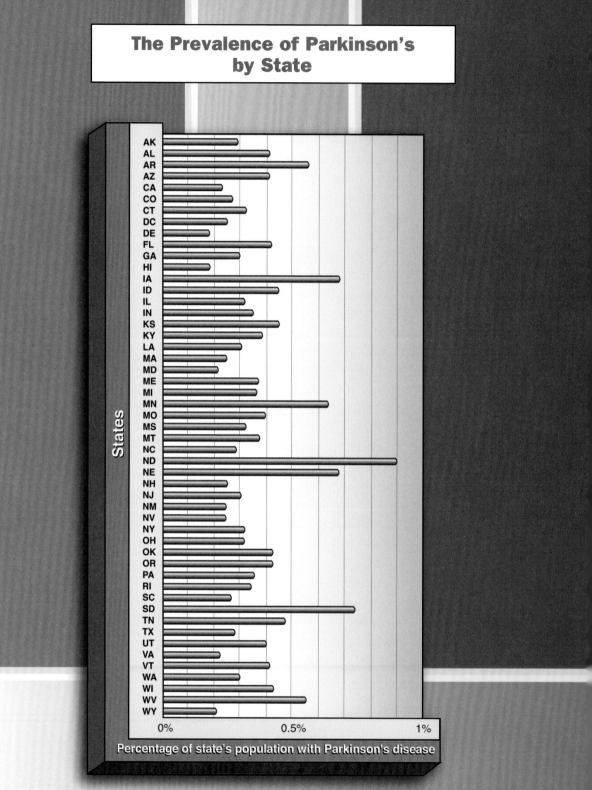

The Prevalence of Parkinson's by State

Percentage of state's population with Parkinson's disease

Taken from: Abraham Lieberman, *Shaking Up Parkinson's Disease: Fighting Like a Tiger, Thinking Like a Fox.* Sudbury, MA: Jones and Bartlett, 2002.

National Institutes of Health for 30 years, Meshul said. Researchers found that animals whose calorie intake was lowered by 20 percent aged better, suffered from fewer immunological disorders, displayed healthier hair and skin tone, and "looked significantly better than a counterpart that hasn't had a restricted diet."

"They live longer," Meshul said. "It's been known for many, many years that dietary restriction is good."

Scientists already have shown dietary restriction initiated before the onset of early Parkinson's can protect against neurochemical changes in the brain caused by the disease. In 1999, researchers found that mice on restricted diets for three months prior to an early Parkinson's diagnosis lost fewer dopamine-synthesizing neurons.

"There's not as much loss of dopamine if you restrict their diets ahead of time," Meshul noted.

Meshul's lab is finding that dietary restriction isn't the only way to boost neurological function in Parkinson's disease. Early results of another study the group is conducting have shown that rats with 90 percent loss of dopamine in the brain—or full-blown Parkinson's disease —under a four-week exercise regimen can run twice as long as parkinsonian rats that didn't exercise.

"We're trying to make the correlation that exercise definitely helps in terms of the parkinsonian animal and, in fact, in human studies it's been shown that any sort of exercise helps patients," Meshul said.

The dietary restriction study was funded by the U.S. Department of Veterans Affairs.

A High-Fat Diet May Help in the Treatment of Parkinson's Disease

Ben Harder

In the following viewpoint Ben Harder discusses a new diet being tested for neurological disorders such as Parkinson's disease. He talks with Marilyn Deaton, a Parkinson's patient, who describes her month-long extremely high-fat diet. This diet produces an increase in ketone bodies, which can have therapeutic effects. The study showed improvements in balance, tremors, and mood. Harder also describes the downsides of a high-fat diet and other studies related to this kind of regimen, including its success in treating epilepsy. Harder is a science and medical reporter.

For a month that tested her determination, Marilyn Deaton dined on little but fat. The recipes she prepared included eggs baked with gobs of cream cheese, small portions of fish outweighed by butter, oil and mayo, and ground beef mixed with so much heavy cream that it ran a light brown.

SOURCE: Ben Harder, "Some Try Ultra-Fat Diet to Combat Medical Conditions," www.usatoday.com, May 14, 2006. Copyright © 2006, USA Today. Reproduced by permission of the author.

"I can't stand things that are soft and slimy," says Deaton, 60, of New York. She missed "crunchable stuff," such as carrots, she says.

Deaton has Parkinson's disease. The disagreeable diet was an experimental treatment prescribed by her doctors. Four other Parkinson's patients followed the same menu.

The results, which included modest improvements in balance, tremors and mood, were encouraging but too preliminary to prove an effect, says Theodore VanItallie of St. Luke's–Roosevelt Hospital Center in New York, VanItallie and his colleagues published their findings [in 2005] in the journal *Neurology*.

Low-Protein Diet Helps Symptoms

Their trial and other recent studies hint that a diet nearly devoid of protein and carbohydrates might temper symptoms of several neurodegenerative disorders, including Alzheimer's and Lou Gehrig's disease, VanItallie says.

Researchers suspect that such a high-fat diet also could stall brain tumors and help patients with certain other health problems—if it doesn't cause strokes along the way.

Though such a solution may sound far-fetched, a similar diet has been used since the 1920s to treat severe epilepsy. Numerous studies, most of them in children who had exhausted other options, have since found that it reduces seizures.

There's scant clinical evidence to address whether the plan, called the ketogenic diet, has wider therapeutic promise. Researchers aren't sure how it works against epilepsy, and they hold various theories about why it might, or might not, help in other disorders.

Some of the benefits result from a shift in the brain's metabolism from blood sugar, the body's main fuel, to ketone bodies, a secondary energy source that is a byproduct of fat metabolism, says Richard Veech, a physician and biochemist with the National Institutes of Health in Bethesda, [Maryland].

But, Veech says, "while VanItallie has shown that (the ketogenic diet) works, as a practical matter, one can't recommend it."

The Obvious Downside

Consequences of high fat intake, heart problems for one, could offset the diet's hypothetical benefits in some people, Veech says. In any case, the daunting challenge of maintaining the unpalatable regimen makes it unlikely to catch on.

"Most people would have a very hard time following this diet," says Cathy Nonas, the dietitian at North General Hospital in New York who designed Deaton's plan. The plan requires that 90% of the patients' calories come from fat and just 8% from protein. In the average American diet, fat makes up 33% of calories, and protein accounts for 15%.

When a person fasts or subsists mainly on fat, blood sugar declines. The liver responds by converting fatty acids into ketone bodies, which normally circulate in the blood at low levels, rising as time passes since a person's most recent meal, when glucose is abundant.

Popular low-carb diets, such as Atkins, may generate some ketone bodies, but not necessarily enough to have a therapeutic benefit, VanItallie says.

Ketone bodies can accumulate to dangerous levels, in diabetics, for example, and turn the blood acidic. But moderately elevated levels are theoretically beneficial in a range of circumstances, Veech says.

Increased Ketone Levels Have Their Advantages

Lab studies and a few desperate medical cases lend some support to that notion. For example, when added to intravenous resuscitation fluids in place of a typical ingredient, ketone bodies also reduce organ damage after major blood loss, says hematologist C. Robert Valeri of the Naval Blood Research Laboratory in Plymouth, [Massachusetts]. He and his colleagues demonstrated that in pigs.

Other teams have shown that the molecules protect mice against neurological changes linked to Parkinson's and Alzheimer's.

[In April 2006], researchers at Mount Sinai School of Medicine in New York reported similar findings for Lou Gehrig's disease, or amyotrophic lateral sclerosis. Giulio Pasinetti of Mount Sinai says his team is launching a trial to treat patients with the disease.

In an older report, a ketogenic diet appeared to slow tumor growth in two children with inoperable brain cancer.

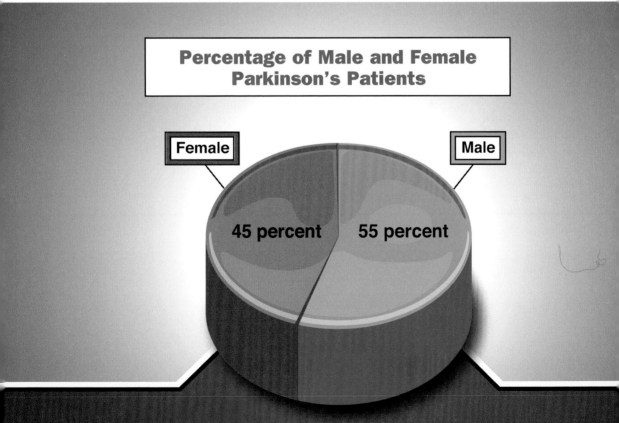

Percentage of Male and Female Parkinson's Patients

Female

45 percent

Male

55 percent

Taken from: Abraham Lieberman, *Shaking Up Parkinson's Disease: Fighting Like a Tiger, Thinking Like a Fox.* Sudbury, MA: Jones and Bartlett, 2002.

Studies have shown that a high-fat diet produces an increase in ketone bodies that can have therapeutic effects on Parkinson's patients. (Image copyright Dusan Zidar, 2009. Used under license from Shutterstock.com.)

Neurobiologist Thomas Seyfried of Boston College later demonstrated the effectiveness of that approach in mice.

Most brain tumor cells, Seyfried says, "can't burn ketones for energy," so elevating ketone levels and simultaneously reducing blood sugar may starve the tumors while nourishing healthy cells.

VanItallie and Nonas are gearing up for a new Parkinson's trial that will test a hybrid of the 90%-fat regimen and the Atkins diet. They've invited their former volunteers to participate.

Deaton says her Parkinson's symptoms improved during the original trial, which was conducted in 2003. And losing 26 pounds was a bonus, she says. But even with a more lenient menu on the table, she doesn't plan on signing up again.

She's trying a more conventional weight-loss plan. It lets her eat carrots.

Embryonic Stem Cells Are More Important than Other Stem Cells in Parkinson's Research

Alix Rogers

In the following viewpoint Alix Rogers argues that embryonic stem cells are worthy of increased funding and study through the federal government. According to Rogers, embryonic stem cells have the potential for use in complicated situations, given enough research time and funding. One concern with restricting embryonic stem cell research in the United States, she says, is that other countries have more opportunities for this type of research, and scientists are leaving the country to pursue research opportunities elsewhere. Rogers also states that the federal government provides a major portion of funding for biomedical research, and adult stem cell research receives a significantly larger amount of monies than embryonic stem cell research. Rogers is a graduate of the University of Pennsylvania and winner of the Gates Cambridge Scholarship.

President George W. Bush has enacted his first ever veto against the bi-partisan bill H.R. 810: The Stem Cell Research Enhancement Act. This bill would

SOURCE: Alix Rogers, "Crib Sheet: Stem Cell Research: What We're Set to Lose from Bush's Veto," *Campus Progress*, July 20, 2006. Copyright © Center for American Progress. This material was created by the Center for American Progress. www.americanprogress.org.

fuel medical research stalled by the [Bush] administration's policy, research which most scientists believe could lead to cures for a wide range of diseases and debilitating conditions, such as paralysis, multiple sclerosis, and Parkinson's Disease. Passed with 63 votes in the Senate and 238 votes in the House, Congress is likely to fall short of the 2/3 majority needed to override a presidential veto. This means that embryonic stem cell research will continue to be hampered across the country.

As young Americans, we should be particularly concerned about this issue. It is one which will ultimately have great impact on us and our health care.

The current policy is preventing cures from being developed, cures which our generation is the most likely to benefit from, because it will be several years before we begin to see clinical applications. Embryonic stem cells could be used to cure a wide variety of diseases including Alzheimer's, diabetes, and spinal cord injuries. A recent Johns Hopkins University study in which researchers used embryonic stem cells to enable paralyzed rats to walk highlights some of the potential medical breakthroughs.

President Bush has claimed that adult stem cells are a more promising avenue of research, because they are already being used in the clinical setting. This argument is absurd in light of the fact that the majority of available treatments involving adult stem cells, such as bone marrow transplants, do not involve complicated attempts to differentiate the cells into specific types of body cells. On the other hand, transforming an embryonic stem cell into a heart or nerve cell is an extremely complicated process that will take substantial time and research—and money. For 2007 the National Institutes of Health (NIH) earmarked only $39 million for human embryonic stem cell (ES) research, while adult stem cell research received

> **FAST FACT**
>
> Embryonic stem cells are derived from eggs that have been fertilized through in vitro fertilization.

$200 million. Adult stem cells have more developed medical applications because they are easier to work with and have received more funding, not because they have more potential. More importantly, an extended time frame is no reason to bar a path of medical research. If we invest in ES research now, it may offer useful treatment by the time members of our generation begin to develop Alzheimer's.

The second problem is that America has a declining crop of researchers and is driving away its best minds.

While president, George W. Bush commented on his decision to veto a bill for embryonic stem cell research, saying it "crosses a moral boundary." **(AP Images)**

Current policies are causing prominent researchers to accept positions in other countries that support their research. Already reports have been issued that show how America is losing its standing in embryonic stem cell research. But what is more disturbing is that many budding scientists are discouraged from entering the field of stem cell research. While testifying to a Senate sub-committee, James Battey, Chair of the NIH Stem Cell Taskforce, said "young people are now electing to stay away from human ES research." Elizabeth Nabel, director of the National Heart, Lung, and Blood Institute, has also said, "The restricted access (to embryonic stem cells) will hamper the NIH's ability to recruit . . . young scientists." This gap is one reason that all of the first round grants given by the state of California as part of its $3 billion investment in stem cell research went to "multi-year training grants to increase the number of young investigators (pre-doctoral, post-doctoral, and clinical fellows) with the technical and academic skills necessary to conduct basic and applied stem cell research." Because young scientists are discouraged from entering the field now, America will have few researchers with the experience and expertise to work with embryonic stem cells, even if the policy is reversed.

So with the potential benefits of pursuing ES research being so great, and the potential costs of not doing so equally significant, why is it so controversial? It's because, despite the fact that human embryonic stem cell research involves a ball of cells in a Petri dish that has no developed nervous system, there are certain groups who believe that the derivation of human embryonic stem cells involves the destruction of nascent human life. So, for the same reason that almost all the same people oppose reproductive freedom for women, they believe embryonic stem cell research should be prohibited (or at a minimum that the government shouldn't fund it.) Seventy-two percent of Americans support embryonic stem cell

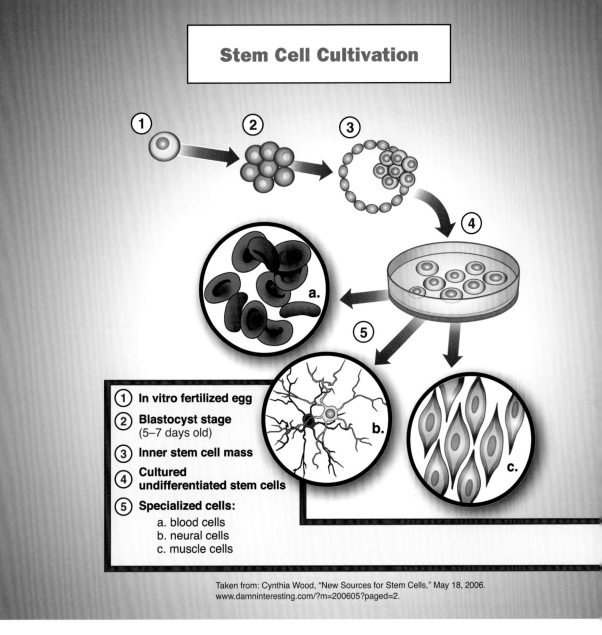

Stem Cell Cultivation

1. **In vitro fertilized egg**
2. **Blastocyst stage** (5–7 days old)
3. **Inner stem cell mass**
4. **Cultured undifferentiated stem cells**
5. **Specialized cells:**
   a. blood cells
   b. neural cells
   c. muscle cells

Taken from: Cynthia Wood, "New Sources for Stem Cells," May 18, 2006. www.damninteresting.com/?m=200605?paged=2.

research, but federal policy is being held hostage by the small minority who oppose it.

On August 9, 2001, President Bush announced his restrictive policy of limiting federal funding for embryonic stem cell research to stem cell lines derived before that day. As science has advanced, it is being increasingly hampered by these conservative policies. Problems such as a lack of access to the federal lines, contamination by mouse feeder cells in which the stem cells grow, and a lack of genetic diversity have plagued federal researchers and caused concern over their ability to use these lines for clinical trials in human patients. These problems are also paired with a general lack of funding for stem cell research by the NIH.

The lack of opportunity, support, and funding provided by the federal government is especially egregious because the federal government is the major funder of basic biomedical research. The NIH received $28.5 billion for 2007 to fund medical research. While states and private industry have taken up some funding of embryonic stem cell research, and they should be commended for doing so, this does not mean they can fill the gap left by the current administration's policy. James Thompson, a stem cell pioneer, has pointed out that "the reality is that the federal government, the National Institutes of Health, is the funding that drives basic research and research into new therapies in this country. And if you exclude that, then you're basically stuck."

For this reason, the issue of stem cells has been bubbling beneath the surface of health discussion in the Senate and the House since 2001, despite President Bush's staunch refusal to reconsider his decision. The most recent passage of H.R. 810 by the Senate represents a break within the Republican Party, as leaders including Senate Majority Leader Bill Frist have come forward in support of embryonic stem cell research. H.R. 810 is a crucial bill, because it would expand the number of embryonic stem cell lines available for federal funding. It would allow funding for research on lines derived from the over 400,000 embryos that are cryogenically frozen and stored in fertility clinics across the country. The vast majority of these embryos will never be implanted in a woman's womb, but will remain indefinitely frozen or simply tossed down a sink. If these embryos are going to be destroyed anyway, should they not be used, with the consent of the donors, for research that could save countless patients whose personhood nobody questions?

Despite pleas by conservatives like [former First Lady] Nancy Reagan and "591 different disease-related groups, patient-advocacy groups, universities, research institutions, renowned scientists, Nobel Prize winners," according to Sen. Tom Harkin (D-Iowa), to support the bill, Bush has adamantly refused to change his stance.

Sen. Orrin Hatch (R-Utah) said before President Bush's veto that "regardless of the president's actions, whether he vetoes this bill or not, we intend to keep pushing this research forward." Pushing this research forward to override a presidential veto will require 50 more House votes and four more Senate votes. As constituents it is our responsibility to apply the necessary pressure on our representatives to encourage them to vote for embryonic stem cell research. We cannot continue to allow Bush to impose a position that flies in the face of science and common sense. To do so would be to deny hope to the millions of patients who are anxiously waiting for the potential of embryonic stem cells to be realized.

[Editor's note: In March 2009, President Barack Obama signed an order that would allow federal funding for embryonic stem cell research, reversing the ban established by his predecessor, George W. Bush.]

Adult Stem Cells Are More Important than Embryonic Stem Cells in Parkinson's Research

Jean Peduzzi-Nelson

In the following viewpoint Jean Peduzzi-Nelson states that the advantages of embryonic stem cells are not as clear as some assert. The rapid cell growth of embryonic cells can cause serious problems and can lead to abnormalities in the chromosomes. Peduzzi-Nelson argues that mature tissue is necessary for testing drug and tissue models. She also states that high rates of rejection can occur with cell transplantation if adult stem cells are not used, and she discusses how adult stem cells affect several different diseases, including Parkinson's. Peduzzi-Nelson is an associate professor of anatomy and cell biology at the Wayne State University School of Medicine.

The great potential moral controversies and political party alignments associated with stem cell issues make the subject a hot topic.

Human stem cells can be obtained from human embryos, produced either by in vitro fertilization of human eggs or cloning via somatic cell nuclear transplant, or adults.

SOURCE: Jean Peduzzi-Nelson, "Adult Stem Cells Are Behind Much of Stem Cell Success So Far," *Milwaukee Journal Sentinel*, September 2, 2006. Reproduced by permission of the author.

The often stated advantages of embryonic stem cells are 1) their great promise, 2) their potential to form every cell type, 3) their rapid proliferation, 4) their lack of rejection and finally, 5) their usefulness in drug testing and disease models.

Embryonic Advantages Are Not Clear

However, from a scientific and medical point of view these advantages are less clear.

The "great promise" of embryonic cells is often stated by scientists that either hold key patents or are strongly supported by biotech companies pursuing embryonic cells commercially.

Every type of stem cell may be useful for injuries but are unlikely to cure most diseases, as underlying causes of uncured diseases are often not known. Stem cells may alleviate the symptoms for several years but not affect the disease process. Other areas of research are actively being studied on disease processes so stem cells are not the magic silver bullet in diseases.

The "potential of embryonic stem cells to possibly form every cell type" in the body is amazing but is of little clinical relevance. As long as a stem/progenitor cell is capable of forming the cell types needed for a particular injury or disease, the capability to form every cell type is a moot point.

Furthermore, there are numerous supporting studies that stem cells derived from adults have the same potential. Sources of adult stem cells include the skin, fat, bone marrow stromal cells, umbilical cord and many other sites in the body.

Embryonic Cells Cause Problems

The "rapid proliferation of embryonic stem cells" is a rather ironic claim in that the quality cited for the superiority of embryonic stem cells is actually responsible for causing serious problems. Rapid growth is not always a desirable quality, as clearly seen with weeds in a garden or cancer in the body.

In an animal model of Parkinson's disease, rats injected with embryonic stem cells showed a slight benefit in about 50% of the rats, but one-fifth of the rats died of brain tumors caused by the embryonic stem cells.

The "lack of rejection of embryonic stem cells" is a clever twist of words. It is true that embryonic cells are not rejected. However, to be useful as a therapy, the cell must mature into a particular cell type. When the cell matures, it is recognized by the immune system as foreign and is rejected. However, it has also been argued that this is the reason for the great need for human cloning (somatic cell nuclear transplant) so the problem of rejection of embryonic stem cells can be avoided.

This field is in its infancy, and only a very few studies have been done to even demonstrate the feasibility of this in experimental animals. Pursuing this extreme measure when the human body is full of stem/progenitor cells that would not be rejected is one of the most absurd directions ever observed in the history of science that is supposedly being promoted to help people.

The Importance of Mature Tissues and Familiar Cells

"Usefulness in drug testing and disease models" is not a reasonable claim because tissue models and drugs need to be tested on mature tissue, not embryonic cells. There are numerous tissue culture model systems of muscle, skin, etc., that are routinely used in drug and disease models. The advantages of stem cells derived from adult stem cells are virtually unknown to the American public. The most profitable, not the best, treatment for people is not surprisingly getting the most publicity.

The greatest advantage of adult stem cells is that it's usually possible to use a person's own stem cells, which is the safest stem cell option for people. This avoids the

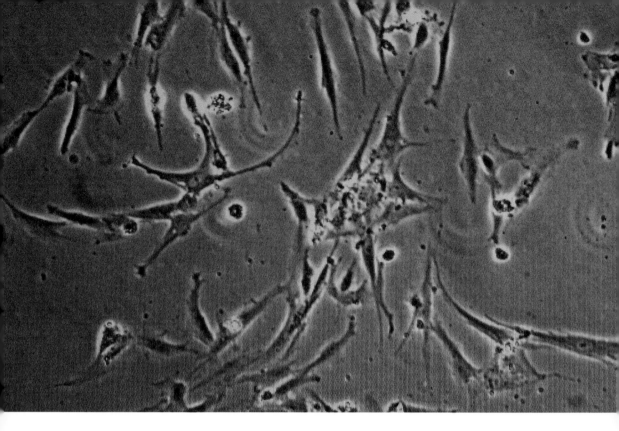

problems of rejection, disease transmission, chromosomal abnormalities and uncontrolled growth.

One problem with embryonic stem cells that is rarely mentioned is that methods have yet to be developed to grow these cells in a manner that does not induce significant chromosomal abnormalities. If one looks at the human clinical trials or research using experimental animals, the record for adult stem cells compared to embryonic stem cells is extremely impressive. In examining only the scientific evidence, one wonders why the controversy even exists.

Adult stem cells are shown in this microscopic view. Some experts maintain that adult stem cells are more effective than embryonic stem cells for Parkinson's research because of their lower rejection rates. (Pat Greenhouse/Boston Globe/Landov)

Stem Cells Work Against a Range of Complications

Parkinson's disease: When a transplant consists of embryonic/fetal tissue, the stem/progenitor cells are the only cells that survive. In two clinical trials using embryonic/fetal tissue, devastating deterioration at one year after treatment occurred in about 15% of these patients that was believed to result from cellular overgrowth or from

Stem Cells Producing Neurons

In a process termed long-term self-renewal, adult stem cells can generate identical copies of themselves over the entire life of an organism, in addition to becoming specialized cells. By contrast, it takes many months of growing embryonic stem cells in a laboratory to see if the stem cell line will have the long-term self-renewal property.

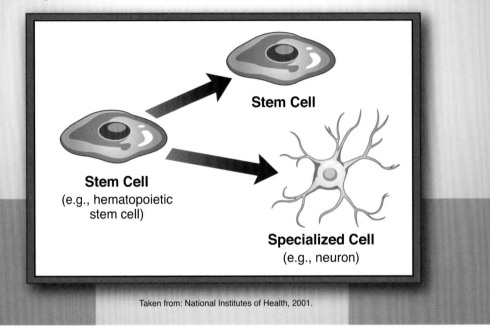

Stem Cell

Stem Cell
(e.g., hematopoietic
stem cell)

Specialized Cell
(e.g., neuron)

Taken from: National Institutes of Health, 2001.

rejection of the foreign cells/tissue derived from embryo or fetus.

These results are in striking contrast to the report on a patient who received his own adult stem cells, who had almost full recovery for several years after the transplant.

In a recent animal study, human embryonic stem cells not only did not cause improvement in an animal model of Parkinson's disease but also caused tumor formation. Another direction of hope for Parkinson's disease is the use of growth factors.

Diabetes: Diabetes, like Parkinson's disease, is a disease, so it may not be possible to cure diabetes with any type of stem cells but only dissipate the symptoms for several years. Recently, insulin independence was reported in a person after receiving cells from her mother.

Also encouraging were results found in animal studies that blocking the autoimmune reaction can reverse diabetes in mice. There are also several reports [that] adult stem cells can develop into insulin-secreting cells.

Spinal cord injury: The comparison of results with adult and embryonic stem cells is even more dramatic. Although mice receiving embryonic stem cells made the front page of many newspapers and extensive web coverage, a paper published by [Mercedes] Zurita and [Jesús] Vaquero found almost total recovery from complete paralysis in rats using adult stem cells from bone marrow. Transplants of tissue containing one's own stem cells is safe and causes some improvement in people with severe, chronic spinal cord injury.

FAST FACT

Adult stem cells are any stem cells obtained after birth.

Heart disease: Several recent studies [of] patients with heart attacks report benefit from adult stem cells derived from bone marrow. Clinical trials have also shown improvements in some patients with heart failure after using one's own adult stem cells in treatment.

Adult Stem Cell Success Is Not Well Known

Similar comparisons can be made for a variety of diseases and injuries. But the successes with adult stem cells will never make headlines or be heard by the majority of the American public.

Although it may take years for these adult stem cell treatments to be commonly available, the results with adult stem cells will eventually end a controversy that should never have existed in the first place. The controversy may end even sooner than that with last month's [August 2006] report that embryonic stem cells can be derived from sperm, as reported in the most recent edition of *Nature.*

CHAPTER 3

The Personal Side of Parkinson's

Laughing with Parkinson's

Stanford Medicine Magazine

Actor Michael J. Fox was diagnosed with Parkinson's disease in 1991 at the age of thirty. In the following viewpoint *Stanford Medicine* interviews Fox about his life with Parkinson's and its effect on his family. Fox discusses misconceptions that people have about the disease as well as the debates surrounding important stem cell research. He also talks about the breakthrough with the growth factor drug GDNF, which has been pulled from testing and is a source of controversy between the drug maker and Parkinson's patients. The Stanford University School of Medicine is an innovative center for biomedical research, and *Stanford Medicine* reports on that research.

W hen it comes to Parkinson's disease [PD], "the science is way ahead of the money," says Michael J. Fox. Though "just" an actor, Fox knows as much about the state of brain disease research as many neuroscientists. He makes it his business now that one of his major pursuits is finding a cure for Parkinson's.

SOURCE: *Stanford Medicine*, "A Conversation with Michael J. Fox," *Stanford Medicine Magazine*, vol. 21, Fall 2004. Copyright © 2004 Stanford University Board of Trustees. Reproduced by permission.

Photo on facing page. A Parkinson's patient kicks a punching bag as part of a workout that has been specifically designed for patients with Parkinson's disease. (Joe Rimkus Jr./MCT/Landov)

Fox gained worldwide popularity in the 1980s with his role as Alex P. Keaton on NBC's *Family Ties*. After this early success, he went on to star in the TV hit *Spin City* and in motion pictures, including the blockbuster *Back to the Future* trilogy, *The American President, Bright Lights Big City* and the "Stuart Little" films, as the voice of the leading mouse.

Though Fox continues to perform occasionally, his priorities changed in 1991 when he was diagnosed with Parkinson's. It's a disease with no known cure. So he founded the Michael J. Fox Foundation for Parkinson's Research, turning his energy to fundraising and grantmaking—all aimed at beating the disease. . . .

Stanford Medicine: Do you get tired of people asking you, "How are you doing?"

Michael J. Fox: No—I understand that it comes from a genuine connection people feel they have with me. So many people tell me, "I grew up with you." Television is such an intimate medium that in a way, they did. So the concern and the connection are very real.

So. How are you doing?

Fine, thanks. . . .

You played a surgeon with obsessive-compulsive disorder on NBC's "Scrubs." Was there any message there?

Not really. It's a funny show and Bill Lawrence, the producer, is a friend of mine. So when he asked me to do it, I said sure. The overall message of the show is a recognition that we're all human, with our individual flaws and foibles, which has an appeal to me. Everyone gets hit with their own bag of hammers at some point in life, you know. And it was just fun.

Discussing Parkinson's with Others

Telling your children that you have a chronic illness must be one of the most difficult discussions a parent ever faces. How do you strike a balance between sharing enough information and sharing too much?

I don't pre-package it for them. I tell the basics in an honest, open way and then let them be with it. What's important for them is not how I feel about having PD, but how they feel about my having PD. I give them reassurance, because I'm a classic optimist, not a fearful person, but it's their experience that matters. It really hasn't been a big thing—they know they can ask me anything anytime—we've got a lot of regular everyday family stuff going on.

Is anger a motivating force or a debilitating one?

I find it neutral and therefore a distraction. It's hard to avoid in the early going but I don't go there much anymore.

Having a chronic illness is pretty serious business. Do you find any humor there?

All the time. I take PD seriously but I rarely take myself seriously. That's the secret.

How has your illness influenced your view of health care in America?

It has made me much more aware of the tremendous financial burden that many people bear. I'm in a pretty privileged position where I don't have to worry about cost of medications, whether I can afford a particular therapy that might help me or whether it's covered by insurance. So many people aren't and have to deal with this financial aspect on top of the illness itself. It's a serious issue in this country.

Things to Know About Parkinson's

What are some of the biggest misconceptions about Parkinson's?

That it is a disease that only affects your grandparents and so somehow is a part of aging. I've met so many people in their 30s, 40s and 50s—baby boomers and younger, who have the disease. It affects their ability to

> **FAST FACT**
>
> Ten percent of Parkinson's patients are forty years old or younger.

be productive in their jobs, in their families, right at the prime of their lives.

Is there any one thing you would like everyone to know about the disease?

People should know that scientists say of all the neurodegenerative diseases, Parkinson's is closest to a cure in our lifetime. I firmly believe this to be true.

Why does progress in biomedical research matter to someone who lives with Parkinson's today?

It matters because we are so close. A focused and forceful effort can improve and/or save the lives of millions of people in the very near future.

Is there anything on the horizon as far as research breakthroughs that particularly excites you?

There's a lot in the pipeline. Our foundation, for example, is leading the search for the first biomarker, or diagnostic test. We thought this was a fishing expedition when we started a year ago [2003]—but preliminary results are really exciting. We're also excited about the progress we see with naturally occurring growth factors—the best known is called GDNF—which appear to protect and rejuvenate the neurons that die in Parkinson's disease. We see breakthroughs in understanding the genetic risk profile of the disease: we're funding the creation of the first gene chip for PD. And of course, while we think cell replacement therapy is further away on the horizon than once thought, it still holds tremendous potential for a cure.

Stem Cells and Parkinson's

How important is stem cell research to the search for treatments and a cure for Parkinson's?

Stem cell research is a critical pathway to a cure in two ways. First, stem cells can be used for cell replacement therapy, to actually produce dopamine neurons that have been lost. There are still quite a few hurdles—the brain is tricky and you'd need to go in without causing damage and figure out how to get the cells to thrive—

but it's tremendously promising. Aside from that, most people don't even focus on something that's perhaps even more important—how critical stem cells are for research. You can't do research on living human neurons. But you can use stem cells to create them and study how they work and the impact of various drugs. It's huge.

Michael J. Fox, who has Parkinson's disease, testifies before the Senate on PD. Fox is a leading advocate of stem cell research and of the use of the banned drug GDNF. (AP Images)

Are you surprised about the intensity of the political debate on stem cell research?

It's nuts. Those of us with Parkinson's and other degenerative diseases see it as so self-defeating. We don't want to clone a Frankenstein or Uncle Charlie so we can play poker with him again. We just want to save lives.

Do you feel as though you are in a race against time?

So many people assume that I'm in this to cure me. While that would be great—and don't get me wrong, having Parkinson's stinks—that's not what this is about. It's like being trapped in a mine with a bunch of people. You don't think, when will I get out. You think, when will we get out. So in that sense, I am impatient. I want all of us to get out.

Besides hurry up and find a cure, is there any other message you would like to share with biomedical researchers?

We recognize that when it comes to Parkinson's disease, the science is way ahead of the money. That's why our foundation is trying to fill the void. So come to us with a "hit it out of the park" idea and if it passes muster, we'll look for a way to make it happen.

Losing the Ability to Dance

Pamela Quinn

Pamela Quinn was a professional dancer when she was diagnosed with Parkinson's disease. Having danced professionally for over twenty years, Quinn describes in the following viewpoint how difficult it was to lose the ability to control her body's movements. While trying to cope with the effects of the disease, Quinn undertook finding out all she could about her condition. During this time she realized that she could help herself and others because of the understanding she had about the body from her years of dance. With the assistance of another dance instructor, Quinn developed a movement class for individuals struggling with Parkinson's.

I was reading the newspaper and it started to flutter, as if moved by a small breeze. But the window wasn't open and the fan wasn't on. Strange, I thought, as I traced the origin of the movement to my left hand.

SOURCE: Pamela Quinn, "Moving Through Parkinson's," *Dance Magazine*, December, 2007, pp. 76–77. Copyright © 2007 MacFadden Dance Magazine, LLC. All rights reserved. Reproduced with the permission of Dance Magazine, Inc.

I watched the hand carefully, without emotion, as it quivered ever so slightly. Had I not been holding the paper, I would not have noticed it at all.

That was the first sign of my Parkinson's disease [PD], which I was diagnosed with two years later at the age of 42. From this small, almost imperceptible beginning, my symptoms grew to where it was difficult to walk across the room without lurching violently from one piece of furniture to the next, grabbing each to stabilize myself.

For anyone, learning that you have a serious illness is a shock. But for a dancer, having a condition that directly affects your ability to move is profoundly shattering. I began dancing when I was in high school. For most of my adolescence and all of my adult life, my world had been centered on class, rehearsal, performance, and teaching. I had been an associate director of ODC [Oberlin Dance Company]/San Francisco for roughly 10 years and collaborated with actor/writer Michael O'Connor on dance and theater works in New York for another 10.

Hiding and Questioning

What lay ahead of me now? Who was I to become? How would I earn my living? I was also a mother and I worried about how I would be able to raise my son. Would I be able to play with him, or even to take care of him physically? In my darkest fantasies I envisioned wheelchairs and nursing homes and physical limitations so severe I would be completely immobilized.

While my symptoms were still mild enough, I tried to hide them. When my left hand trembled, I held it with my right behind my back or crossed my arms in front. If I had to walk with another person I exerted enormous effort to step as evenly as I could, and if they noticed something amiss I excused it as a pulled muscle or sprained ankle. But Parkinson's is a progressive disorder and as time went on it became difficult to mask its effects. I retreated from the dance world, knowing that dancers would be the first to pick up on a movement disorder. I stopped going to class, stopped seeing concerts, and stopped choreographing on other dancers.

This was a period of mourning. At the same time, it was a period of feverish questioning and searching for help. I saw the best neurologist I could find. I saw a nutritionist, an acupuncturist and herbalist, and a movement therapist specializing in Parkinson's—Martha Partridge, masterful practitioner of Trager [an approach to movement education that focuses on mind and body]. At a certain point, I realized I had also been seeing another specialist: myself. Over time I had as a matter of course (as any dancer worth her salt would) been making adaptations, experimenting with ways to alleviate or circumvent my symptoms. If my left hand was in tremor, I learned to calm it by shaking it vigorously. If my left foot dragged, I practiced kicking a soccer ball in a string bag to help it come forward. If my left arm didn't want to move in a full range of motion, I swung my purse from arm to arm to wake it up.

FAST FACT

Tremor is the first symptom in 75 percent of Parkinson's patients.

Eventually I recognized that in addition to the medications I was taking (which are essential), the greatest resource I had was the understanding of the body that my life in dance had given me. Those of us who spend our lives working with the body are learning how to speak to the body: how to question it, coax it, finesse it, scold it, trick it if necessary—like a child for whom we have the utmost tenderness but whom we sometimes must guide. In a crisis of disease, this understanding has the potential to affect the course of our condition.

As this realization gradually crystallized, I began to think of how I might share some of what I had discovered with other Parkinson's patients. I did this with some misgivings at first. Would it be depressing to surround myself with the disease? Could I handle seeing what I might become? But my neurologist (the wonderful Rachel Saunders-Pullman) assured me that, relative to the time I had had the disease, my condition was exceptional. Also I was convinced that movement played a significant role in how my PD had progressed—or, rather, the degree to which its progress had been slowed.

Developing a Movement Lab

After assorted attempts to find a forum to present my ideas, I learned of a dance class at the Mark Morris Dance Center in Brooklyn specifically for people with PD. (More than one person can have a good idea.) The woman who had initiated the class was Olie Westheimer, an inspiring advocate for arts-based therapy and founder of the Brooklyn Parkinson's Group. She was happy to meet another like-minded soul, and I suggested developing a sort of movement laboratory. It would be a place to experiment with movement ideas, a class for those struggling with Parkinson's to challenge themselves and, not incidentally, to have fun doing it. She was game, and I began to put together a warm-up, postural exercises, a mini aerobics section, and movement problems related to PD symptoms, along with several cooperative games.

Contrary to my fears, I found the experience of working with other Parkinson's patients beautifully invigorating. The people who come have a wide range of conditions, from relatively functional to those who struggle mightily to take a step in an upright position. But it is enormously moving to see each individual confront their limitations and search their way through or around or over them. I sense the pleasure in the room when we move to the rhythm of our percussionist (the stellar Tigger Benford), and the delight in the giddy tension our ball-throwing games create.

Parkinson's disease is horrible and very frustrating. I do not wish it on anyone. That said, something deeply satisfying has also come from it. Were I never to have had

this challenge, I would never have had the opportunity to understand the ways in which my training and experience fortified me for it, and I would never be communicating my own discoveries about the resilience of our capacities for movement to others. In that respect, my understanding of movement, of the dynamic use of the muscles particular to dance, is deeper now. My disease took dance from me, but in another way gave it back. For that I will, with a rueful shake of my head and the sound of that rattling paper in my mind, give thanks. I'm dancing still.

An elderly couple in which the husband suffers from Parkinson's participated in a recent medical study that had patients dancing the tango as part of their therapy. (Huy R. Mach/ MCT/Landov)

Participating in a Controlled Study of Parkinson's

Lynda McKenzie, as told to Barbara Blake-Krebs and Linda Herman

In the following viewpoint Barbara Blake-Krebs and Linda Herman present Lynda McKenzie's account of her participation in a controlled study of Parkinson's disease involving fetal cell transplantation. In 1996 Lynda McKenzie underwent brain surgery to transplant fetal cells, in the hope that the cells would grow in the brain and relieve some of the symptoms of her disease. At the time of the surgery, McKenzie did not know if she would be receiving the cell transplant or would be a control subject, someone who undergoes the surgery without receiving any treatment. Lynda describes her experiences with the study and the outcomes over the course of four years. Blake-Krebs is a writer and educator. Herman is a technical services librarian and researcher. Both women have Parkinson's disease.

SOURCE: *When Parkinson's Strikes Early: Voices, Choices, Resources and Treatment.* © 2001 by Barbara Blake-Krebs and Linda Herman. To order, call (800) 266-5592, fax (510) 865-4295, or visit the Hunter House Web site at www.hunterhouse.com.

Lynda McKenzie, a 46-year-old artist from Ontario, Canada, was diagnosed with Parkinson's disease [PD] in 1987. The disease progressed to the advanced stage, and Lynda was becoming increasingly disabled, unable even to get out of bed by herself. She was also suffering from severe dyskinesia and injuries from frequent falls. She took part in a 1996 clinical trial of fetal cell transplantation at the University of Colorado in Denver, knowing that according to the research protocol, she had a 50 percent chance of receiving an actual transplant and a 50 percent chance of receiving sham brain surgery.

The Presurgery Experience from McKenzie's Perspective

Waiting for the phone to ring. After returning home from my last pre-op tests in New York, life became a waiting game. The phone call that would summon us to Denver for surgery would come on a Monday. Two days later, we would have to be on our way to the University of Denver, where the double-blind surgery would take place early Thursday morning. Each Monday I stayed close to home, jumping every time the phone gave its specially coded long-distance ring. Four Mondays passed that way. On the fifth, at just before 5:00 P.M., as I told myself all the good reasons why we would be waiting another week, the phone rang. Long distance. "Mrs. McKenzie? Your surgery is scheduled for this Thursday."

Thursday, University of Denver Hospital. "Good morning, Mrs. McKenzie. We're ready to start preparing you for surgery." Al [McKenzie's husband] came into my room and gave me a big hug. Behind him were Dr. Breeze and three nurses pushing a metal cart loaded with my halo, assorted hardware, needles, vials, and a Black and Decker drill.

Dr. Breeze introduced himself and explained calmly that the next few minutes would be the worst part of the whole procedure. Before I had a chance to dwell on that, they lowered the large medieval-looking stereotactic device (halo) over my head until the lower horizontal bars reached my nose. They then positioned the upper circular bar on my forehead. Dr. Breeze used a black magic marker to indicate the positions of the four screws that would hold the halo to my skull. Dr. Breeze filled several giant needles from a vial on the cart and dabbed a topical freezing solution on the four insertion points.

Inserting the Halo

With one nurse holding my shoulders, another holding my head, and Al clutching my hands, Dr. Breeze inserted the first long needle into my forehead. The liquid burned. There's not a lot of flesh in that area, and he was right, it did hurt. Quickly he picked up a fresh needle and insert-ed it on the other side of my forehead. Two more needles in the back of my head and the halo was lowered into place. A few brackets were tightened so it fit as snugly as possible. Even though I had confidence in Dr. Breeze, the sight of his Black and Decker drill poised at my forehead was frightening.

"This tool does the best job I've found; the initial contact of the screw might hurt a bit, but when it gets past a certain area, it won't hurt any more." The nurses tightened their grips and he squeezed the power switch to "on." Initially, it felt like the sharp cut of a large knife, but it did ease up a bit. I heard the drill stop and start twice and felt his hand on the back of my head.

Then he positioned the drill over my right forehead and turned it on. This time the pain was incredible. I squeezed Al's hand and tears ran down my cheeks. I in-stinctively pulled back but the nurses held me, and all I could do was cry, "It hurts, it really, really hurts." It seemed an eternity before the drill stopped. Not realizing that the screws had already been inserted and tightened on the back, I remember thinking there was no way I could go through that pain again. If only there were a way to leap out of bed and run down the hall to *anywhere* else. Unfortunately, my traitor of a body was sufficiently cobbled by lack of medication and nurses that escaping wasn't an option.

The Oldest Joke in the World

The next challenge was to move my motionless body, complete with heavy metal cage, from bed to stretcher. Finally, propped with pillows under my neck, I was rolled out of the room past my roomie, Joy. She must have wondered what ancient form of torture had been going on behind the curtain. As I rolled by her, I couldn't resist saying, "I bet you wish you had one of these too, eh, Joy!"

I was wheeled to the operating room. Nurses, technicians, surgeons were gowned and gloved. Everyone was ready for Dr. Breeze's arrival. While we waited, eyes

As part of a 1996 clinical trial, a number of Parkinson's patients underwent surgery for fetal cell transplantation, as shown in the surgical procedure pictured here. (Phanie/Photo Researchers, Inc.)

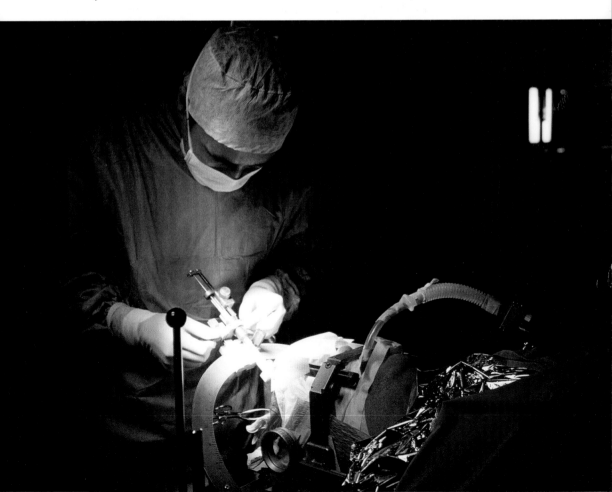

peered down at me over green facemasks, and voices muffled by surgical masks introduced themselves.

"Hi, Lynda. I'm Sue. I'll be with you throughout the surgery."

"Don't worry, Lynda, you'll be up and moving soon."

"Hi, Lynda. I'm Frank. I'll be checking your blood pressure."

At that moment, I thought of a favorite joke of my dad's. It would be perfect for this moment! I couldn't let the opportunity go by. "Frank, now that we're in Denver, you know, near all those wonderful ski resorts, when this surgery is over, will I be able to ski?" Frank took my hand and quickly assured me that of course I would!

"Wow, that's great Frank! Because you know something, I never could get the hang of it before!"

Everyone in the room groaned; they'd been caught by one of the oldest jokes in the world! I contentedly rested on my laurels, thinking proudly how I'd aced the delivery of the joke even in my groggy state.

Suddenly, it was time to go into the operating room. Everyone sprang into action. The gurney began to move and Al kissed me. I was quickly wheeled into the operating room and transferred to a cold, hard table. Bolts held my halo to the table. I was totally immobile and immovable. I forced myself to keep awake and watch the activity in the room. All were focused on me and my failing brain. I focused on everyone who has Parkinson's now and everyone who will be diagnosed with it before the cause and cure are finally found. The bustling, blurry movement around me was almost dreamlike.

Finally. A year of medical questionnaires, videos, grueling tests, tears, and hopes. I firmly believed that within the hour the fetal tissue would be safely implanted in my brain. Because of my optimism, I wasn't frightened at all.

FAST FACT

More than two hundred Parkinson's patients have had surgery involving tissue transplant.

I confidently placed my future in the hands of everyone in that room.

Sham Surgery

In spite of Lynda's optimism, she learned a year later that she had been in the control group and had not received a transplant. In order to rule out a placebo effect, the researchers sought to compare results of surgery with implants against fake or "sham" surgery. Lynda and nineteen other participants had holes drilled in their heads but did not receive cell transplants during the surgery.

For a few months, Lynda said she actually felt some improvement, but it was short lasting, and after about 4 months, she realized her symptoms were worsening. She was relieved to learn at the end of the year that she hadn't received the implant—this meant that her hope for improvement was still alive. As part of the research protocol she was given the opportunity to receive actual implant surgery, which took place about 2 years later, in 1998.

Promising Results: The Basis for More Research

Lynda wrote in July 1999:

Good news from New York!

Just want to let everyone know about the get-together at Columbia Presbyterian in New York City on Sunday afternoon, July 11th. It was for all the people who are participating in Drs. Freed and Fahn's fetal-transplant study. Finally, after being cautioned against talking with each other before the results were released, we were invited to get together to meet and hear the latest results.

Although the results in general seem to be better for those under age 60, they did speak of good results happening for the over-60 group, but at a slower rate. One 75-year-old man experienced very good results, they said.

Out of 19 who received the "right" surgery the first time, one person is off meds altogether and three are taking very small amounts now. The greatest improvements occur at the 12- to 18-month post-op time and continue from there.

PET [positron-emission tomography] scans show that all transplanted cells *did* grow in the recipient's brain. Why they work better in some than in others is a good question and will hopefully be the basis for one of the next studies.

Dr. Freed said he had hoped this surgery would be the answer to PD. Instead of feeling that his hopes for a medical miracle weren't realized, he knows that so much valuable information has been obtained and is already being used for future research.

I had the opportunity to see the doctors and nurses who have worked so hard to make this study work. They are dedicated, caring, and wonderful people who only want to see PD ended. I have the utmost respect for them and always will. I say "thank you" to them every time I get out of bed by myself, turn over in bed *all by myself*, and accomplish those little things taken for granted by so many.

Symptoms Have Lessened

Lynda McKenzie wrote on 26 October 1999:

It has been almost a year since the "real" surgery for me (December 1998). The majority of my days are "on" now, as opposed to this time last year when the majority were "off." Since February, I haven't had the incredible dystonia I once had.

The past 2 weeks have been a whirlwind for me; in fact, the past few months have just flown by! We have traveled to Vancouver, Nova Scotia, Maine, New York City, Montréal, and Ottawa. I have been interviewed on numerous TV stations here in Canada, as well as many radio shows.

I have resumed driving, and no longer have that awful feeling wondering if even if I get there, will I get home? Dyskinesia has decreased as well; my bruises are actually healing and not being replaced! I know that the positive results from the surgery weren't as quick as I'd hoped (we all have our dreams), but now, looking back on the past year, they are definitely here.

I feel as though I've been given a second chance. Each day is a new discovery, and I look forward to continuing to improve.

I know that the surgery I had is not the cure, or even the perfect solution for everyone, but it is an important step on the way. I want to be part of the solution, and not being a doctor or a scientist or a researcher, I feel that I can do my part by giving PD some visibility. I really want to keep hope alive, and I believe that by getting out there and speaking, and increasing awareness, I can do that.

A Step in the Right Direction

A letter from Lynda [in] August 2000:

Al and I just returned from my 18-month post-op tests in New York City. The news is not particularly earth-shattering on that front. As the results continue to be tallied from the remaining participants, it is becoming more and more obvious that the fetal tissue implant surgery is just a step in the right direction, not an end in itself.

Granted, some people are feeling better, and that is wonderful. I wish I were one of those who are sure they improved measurably. I do know that now the pressure is off and people aren't looking for me to show up one day completely cured. . . . My physical symptoms are as manageable as 13-year-old Parkinson's can be, but the remarkable thing is my emotional well-being. And that is just as good, if not better than ever. There is no need for me to second guess every tremor, every episode of dyskinesia or rigidity, as to why? How? Or when? They just are. That also doesn't mean I never get frustrated, or upset, or cry. I do. But that's all right, because it's part of the package. A package I can accept and deal with. It isn't what I'd wish for in a perfect world, but it's okay and it's me.

As Al and I retrieved our car from the hospital parking lot and deposited our bags inside, we realized that it was exactly 4 years ago, almost to the day, that we were there for my very first series of tests after being accepted into the study. How excited and full of promise we both felt then! I was positive that this procedure would provide the "out" for me from the clutches of this disease. I also was so sure I would receive the right tissue the first time. I kept picturing myself whizzing through the tests, astounding everyone with my vast improvement and ultimately becoming a spokesperson for the procedure.

However, so far, I have to admit that some things, no matter how badly you want them, are just not meant to be. . . .

Publishing Test Results

In March 2001, the results of this pioneering study were published in the *New England Journal of Medicine*. The researchers found evidence that transplanted embryonic neurons survived in the brains of a majority of the subjects of all ages; however, measurable clinical benefits were realized only by patients under 60 years old. The researchers concluded that surgical techniques needed further refinement, due to the occurrence of serious dystonia and dyskinesia in five patients receiving the transplants.

Dr. Freed indicated that the research ". . . will continue, for we now have a base of experience. . . . This research is an important milepost for the ongoing development of cell transplantation as a treatment for Parkinson's. We are now testing ways to produce a better and more uniform response in individual patients."

Although there were some negative reports in the mass media, calling the fetal tissue transplant study a "failure," Lynda McKenzie did not share that viewpoint. She stated, "When people look at me now and hear that I was part of Dr. Freed's study, I can see them shake their heads as they think 'Hmm, so that was obviously a waste of time' and 'those poor patients who were given those promises and false hopes.' Wrong, wrong, wrong! First of all, who knows what we would be like now had we not been part of the study. Secondly, look how much we learned to enable us to go on to subsequent studies."

Lynda also indicated if given the opportunity, she would have the transplant treatment all over again, and she looks forward to the future and the promise of a cure for Parkinson's. . . .

Lynda Writes Again

The past 4 years have been the most incredible 4 years of my life! So much has happened! So many doors have opened, I've met so many wonderful people, so many roadblocks have turned into opportunities—how could I even dare to wish it hadn't happened? If I were given a chance to relive these past 4 years, would I have chosen any differently? Nope. I'd do it again in a minute.

This summer finds me busy with many things. I'm exploring several alternative methods of dealing with Parkinson's, including a type of Reiki [a spiritual practice], massage, regular exercise, meditation, neurofeedback, nutrition, visiting special friends, and just chillin' out. Maybe that's why I'm feeling pretty good.

Even though part of my brain has suffered from corporate downsizing in the dopamine department, I'm convinced that there is some other course (or courses) of action excitedly waiting in the wings. Because I'm the way I am, I'd like to be there when it makes its debut.

Given the choice of being a realist who slams the door shut, lamenting that something "probably won't work," or an optimist who opens the door with a wide welcome and sees how it *could* work, I know what I'll continue to pick.

Being Diagnosed with Parkinson's

Glenna Wotton Atwood

In 1981 at the age of forty-seven, Glenna Wotton Atwood was diagnosed with Parkinson's disease after having noticed symptoms more than two years earlier. At that time, not much was known about the disease and she was told by more than one doctor to keep her condition secret. In the following viewpoint Atwood describes her search for information about the disease and for a specialist who understood Parkinson's. She also discusses the importance of finding a doctor she felt comfortable with and one who would be completely honest with her about the disease. Almost thirty years after her diagnosis, Atwood is still active.

Life was beautiful in 1978. My marriage was solid, and my husband and I felt better than ever about our relationship. We were pleased with our children, now grown and married to individuals whom we

SOURCE: Glenna Wotton Atwood, *Living Well with Parkinson's.* Oxford, UK: John Wiley and Sons, 2005. Copyright © 1991, 2005 by Glenna Wotton Atwood, Lila Green Hunnewell, and Roxanne Moore Saucier. All rights reserved. Reproduced by permission of Blackwell Publishers.

loved dearly. My career as an educator was at its peak, and I felt very productive. I was forty-seven years old. Physically, I had never felt better. I had wonderful friends and relatives. I had a lovely home in Maine. Is it any wonder that I did not want anything to disturb my life?

Glenna Wotton Atwood's History

I was born Glenna Wotton in 1931, in a small community in northern Maine. I grew up during the Depression years, surrounded by relatives who were short on money but never short on love and caring for one another. Mine was a secure world, where life revolved around the one-room school, the church, and my family. Eventually, when I left home to become a teacher, I was armed with faith and the values with which I had grown up.

At the University of Maine in Farmington, I earned my B.S. in Home Economics, and I met Blaine Atwood, who was also preparing to teach. We married and settled in Hampden, not far from Bangor, and near Orono, where we could continue our education while we taught school. Eventually, I became a teacher and then the chairman of the Home Economics Department of Hampden Academy.

Those were active, exciting years. I expanded the home economics program to include courses in consumer education, independent living, family life, and child development, and I started a nursery school within the department. The Maine Department of Education was using some of my courses as models, and other school systems in Maine, other states, and even other nations, were adapting my course, "Independent Living." It was a good feeling to be contacted by people who wanted to use my ideas. In 1975, I was named Maine's "Home Economics Teacher of the Year."

I looked forward to a blissful future. There were so many things to enjoy and accomplish. For one thing, I assumed we would have grandchildren. I planned to be the happiest, peppiest grandmother: my grandchildren would never have to deal with a grumpy, pokey old lady. I would retire early from the school system and embark on an enterprise of my own. I considered many possibilities. I could run my own school, where there would be no bells to require my students to jump up and leave before they were ready. I could start a day-care center based on ideas I believed in. I had ideas for at least fifty pursuits, but I hadn't made a choice. I felt that, eventually, God would help me choose.

Things Start to Change

Was it on July 3, 1978, on December 24, 1979, or on some other date that I first felt a change? I really can't say. I do know that "it" sneaked up on me as I went on my way. Once in a while, my right arm felt clumsy as I walked or stood, as if I didn't know what to do with it. But I ignored it. Doesn't everyone feel a bit awkward once in a while? At times, Blaine lost patience with my pace when we were walking and asked me to speed up. He complained that if he slowed down for me, I would slow down even more. I assumed that this was Blaine's problem, not mine: he was always in a hurry.

> **FAST FACT**
>
> The onset of Parkinson's disease may occur five to ten years before symptoms appear.

Then one day in the summer of 1980, while I was writing a letter to my daughter, Susan, my fingers became balky. The smooth flow of my writing was lost. I was annoyed but said nothing. This feeling in my hands did not go away, and it took me longer and longer to write anything. Sometimes I had to draw the letters or print. My letter-writing habits began to change: I wrote shorter and shorter letters. But I thought, "Ignore this change! Eventually, it will go away."

School reopened, and things were almost back to normal, yet I continued to be nagged by physical problems: Why was I getting so tired? Why was I really dragging by noon? What were the weird sensations I felt from time to time? My legs especially seemed to feel strange and heavy: they jerked or felt as if a rubber band were around them. But I felt that I must not complain; if I didn't tell anyone, these sensations would go away. I remembered the time, many years ago, when I learned that my fifteen-month-old niece had been struck and killed by a car, I had *screamed,* telling myself that if I screamed loudly enough, the news would not be true. This time I hoped that silence would work. Although I had spent years teaching students to be open about their feelings, I kept all this to myself.

Flu Is Not the Problem

Early in 1981, I caught the flu. My recovery was very slow, and finally my daughter, Susan, and my husband, Blaine, insisted that I go to a doctor. Coincidentally, I had just been reading a medical column in the daily newspaper, in which a reader had asked about the symptoms of Parkinson's disease. The doctor's answer described my symptoms: "The earliest signs are apt to be a difficulty in handwriting, a slight trembling of the hand, and a jackknife effect when you put two fingers together." Overcome by anxiety, I knew, but I still didn't tell anyone about my symptoms. I still hoped I was wrong. Yet I knew the time had come to see a doctor. Without telling my family, I admitted to myself that the problem was bigger than a simple case of the flu. One thing at a time.

I made an appointment for March 30 with my family doctor. After the usual physical examination and discussion of my symptoms, my doctor said he suspected I might have Parkinson's disease. He happened to have a young student doctor in his office who was preparing to specialize in neurology. My doctor called him in, told him my symptoms, and said he suspected Parkinson's. The student observed my tremor and asked me to walk. My walk was awkward, and my arm swing was almost nonexistent. His statement was cold and brief: "That isn't

Parkinson's. The tremor is too fine. I'd say it's more likely to be a tumor on the brain." With that, he left. I do not know his name, but whoever he is, and wherever he is, I hope he has learned a great deal more about diagnosing Parkinson's and about dealing with patients.

In the absence of any definitive diagnostic test for Parkinson's, my doctor called to make an appointment for me with a neurologist in Bangor. But this was March, and the neurologist couldn't give me an appointment until July. After all, what's a three- or four-month delay when you are waiting to hear whether you have Parkinson's disease or a brain tumor?

Blaine and I were thankful that my doctor did not want to wait until July. He offered to contact a neurologist in Boston, if we were willing to travel that far. We were, and an appointment in Boston was made for the following week.

During that week, we tried to go on as usual, to work, to sleep, and to eat. At the time, one of our very dear friends was dying of a cancerous tumor on the brain, and our anxiety about the possibility of a tumor on my brain was almost unbearable.

No One Needs to Know

Blaine and I took Friday off and journeyed to Boston to see my first neurologist. This doctor was a mature man and had no doubt seen many people with Parkinson's in his day. He was kind, gentle, and unhurried. We sensed that he was reluctant to tell us his diagnosis. At last, he told us that I was in the mild stages of Parkinson's disease and that it would take about ten years for me to enter the advanced stages. He advised me to go home, go back to work, and tell no one; no one would know. He told me nothing about medication, about what I would look and feel like in ten years, or about where I might get more information. And he did not explain why I should keep the diagnosis a secret.

Actually, we paid little attention to those mysteries at the moment. Blaine and I were too happy that the diagnosis was Parkinson's and not a brain tumor. At least Parkinson's wouldn't kill me. We wept with relief.

In the next weeks, I underwent CAT [computerized axial tomography] scans and other diagnostic tests to rule out other medical problems. At last my family doctor, who reviewed the tests, said that the results supported the neurologist's diagnosis. He agreed with the neurologist that I should exercise, keep up my good attitude, and keep on working. He, too, felt that I should tell no one and that no one need know.

Looking for Answers

I should have asked for more information, but my generation had been conditioned not to question the doctor; we'd learned to sit and agree to do what the doctor tells us to do. One thing I would have liked to know was why I shouldn't tell anyone. I realize that some patients really may not want to know any more than what the doctor tells them, but I was anxious to educate myself about this illness that had taken up residence in my body. I knew that it was progressive and that there was no cure. I knew a little about how the tremor acted, how one muscle worked against the other, how a person looked shuffling along all bent over. But that was all I knew.

I soon discovered that it would be difficult to educate myself: very little information was available, and I didn't know anyone else who had Parkinson's disease. Finally, Blaine learned of Merle Watson, a Parkinson's patient who lives in a neighboring town. I called Merle's wife, Barbara, and she gave me the addresses of the four national organizations concerned with Parkinson's disease. Their free materials, which I obtained in the mail, seemed to be the extent of the information available to patients in 1981. These depressing materials contained pictures of people with frozen facial expressions and thin, bent-over figures. Very little in the materials could give me much hope that I might live in reasonable comfort, as I later learned to live. However, I was now on several mailing lists, and soon newsletters began to appear. Within a year, more was being written, and what was written was more positive. (Although Parkinson's was not at the top of the researchers' lists when my disease was diagnosed, a renewed interest in Parkinson's generated much more research in subsequent years.)

By 1982, I knew I was going to retire from teaching. I had shared my "secret" of Parkinson's disease with my students and colleagues, as well as with my family and friends, and they were all very helpful. But it was not fair to have others do my work. Also, no matter how much they did, they could not take away the pain in my hips that made me limp, the all-over aching, and the extreme tiredness that kept me on the couch from the time I got home until bedtime.

Atwood Seeks an Expert

It was frustrating that no one seemed to understand Parkinson's disease. The feeling kept growing in me that I needed to find an expert in the field. I learned the name of another neurologist, and in February 1982, I visited my second specialist. He, too, was helpful and understanding, and I certainly could not find any fault with him. But what I was really looking for was a specialist who lived and breathed Parkinson's disease. My family doctor and the neurologist had so many other illnesses to deal with. The question kept recurring in my mind: how much time do they really have to keep up with the latest findings on one disease—Parkinson's?

Finding my specialist in Parkinson's disease happened in a roundabout way. Blaine and I began thinking that we might start a Parkinson's support group in our area. We needed to talk to others with Parkinson's and felt that people in our area must have the same need. One

person we talked to was Mary Dike of Gardiner, Maine, whom we contacted after reading about her in a newspaper article. Mary was also interested in starting a support group in her area. A home economics teacher a few years younger than I, Mary was about to leave teaching because of Parkinson's disease. She told us about her doctor, Robert Feldman, a Parkinson's specialist at Boston Medical Center. Listening to Mary, I felt that I had found the specialist I was looking for.

We made an appointment, and on April 2, 1983, I saw my third neurologist, Dr. Feldman. We were not disappointed. We found him and his multidisciplinary team to be experts whose aim was to educate the patient about Parkinson's disease and who knew how to treat the disease. They drew Blaine, me, and our family doctor into the "team." During that visit and at subsequent visits every six months, Dr. Feldman, Blaine, and I talked

An elderly Parkinson's patient consults with his doctor. To manage their treatment responsibly, Parkinson's patients should not hesitate to ask questions of the doctors who treat them. (Simon Fraser/ RVI/Newcastle upon Tyne/Photo Researchers, Inc.)

together until we agreed on a course of treatment that was satisfactory to all of us. Then Dr. Feldman wrote to our family doctor advising him of the results of our meeting This is the pattern we still follow. Thus, I have the security of knowing that if I have any immediate problems, my family doctor, close by, knows my status.

A Patient's Responsibilities

I had come a long way since I first responded to my symptoms in 1980. I learned that I needed to take the responsibility of keeping myself as healthy as possible and to ask questions in the doctor's office. I learned that doctors, too, are human: some find it difficult to say, "I don't know," when they can't diagnose an illness. Some find it difficult to tell the patient when they do know. Some are insensitive. All doctors are different, just as all patients are different. It's important to find the right combination.

I feel that our persistence in looking for the right specialist has paid off. We feel good about our team.

GLOSSARY

acetylcholine   A neurotransmitter for cholinergic neurons, which are involved in motor function along with other functions.

action tremor   This type of tremor occurs with any movement in an affected body part. Action tremors include postural tremor, task-specific tremor, and kinetic tremor.

akinesia   The absence of body movement.

amantadine   This drug has been found to control dyskinesia and is also used to treat bradykinesia, tremors, and rigidity. It was first developed to treat influenza.

apomorphine   A derivative of morphine that is used to treat freezing episodes in severe Parkinson's cases.

basal ganglia   Type of brain cells in the inner part of the brain that produce the chemical dopamine. Through dopamine, the basal ganglia control movement of the body.

bradykinesia   Slow movement of the body or certain areas of the body.

carbidopa   Chemical that prevents the breakdown of levodopa before it reaches the brain; found in combined carbidopa-levodopa medications such as Sinemet.

continuous dopaminergic stimulation (CDS)   Using a long-acting dopamine medication to help treat and control motor complications resulting from long-term use of levodopa.

corpus stratum   The area of the brain that controls movement, including walking and balance.

dardarin	Protein associated with mutations in the gene LRRK2, providing a familial link to Parkinson's. The name is derived from the Basque word for tremor, *dardara*.
deep brain stimulation	A surgical technique involving electrodes that send electrical impulses to certain areas of the brain to help control symptoms of Parkinson's disease.
DJ-1	Gene associated with early-onset Parkinson's disease.
dopamine	The main neurotransmitter affected by Parkinson's. This chemical decreases over time, leading to the symptoms of the disease.
dopamine agonist	Medications that mimic the brain chemical dopamine.
dopaminergic	Anything related to the neurotransmitter dopamine.
dyskinesia	Irregular or abnormal writhing of voluntary muscles.
dystonia	Involuntary muscle spasms or contractions that cause irregular movements. This is often tied to long-term drug treatment for Parkinson's.
freezing	The involuntary inability to move. This Parkinson's symptom is temporary, but there is no way to tell how long a freezing episode will last.
homocysteine	This amino acid is used to build proteins in the body and may contribute to the formation of Lewy bodies.
hypokinesia	Unusually diminished motor activity.
kinetic tremor	Occurs during purposeful voluntary movement.
L-dopa	A naturally occurring amino acid found in food that is converted into dopamine in the brain and body. When produced synthetically, it is used to treat the symptoms of Parkinson's. The scientific drug name is L-3,4-dihydroxyphenylalanine.

levodopa One of the main drugs used to treat the symptoms of Parkinson's. The drug is used to replace missing dopamine in the brain. It is often given in conjunction with the medication carbidopa. Also known as L-dopa.

Lewy bodies Protein deposits that appear in dead or dying neurons that produce dopamine. Lewy bodies are one of the main elements of Parkinson's.

MPTP An environmental toxin injected by drug addicts in the 1980s as synthetic heroin. The resulting illness symptoms were very similar to those of Parkinson's disease.

neuron A nervous system cell that conducts impulses to the brain, nerves, or spinal column.

neurotransmitter A chemical in the brain that transmits or inhibits nerve impulses at the synapse.

pallidotomy Brain surgery that destroys a part of the brain by forming an irreversible lesion on the globus pallidus to help control Parkinson's symptoms.

paraesthesia An abnormal sensation in the body, often causing numbness and tingling in the hands, feet, arms, and legs.

postural deformity Having stooped posture.

postural instability Having difficulty with balance.

postural tremor Having increased tremors of the arms when hands are stretched out in front of the body.

rigidity A stiffness or immobility of the muscles associated with Parkinson's.

rotenone An environmental toxin used to control nuisance fish in lakes that has been linked to Parkinson's disease symptoms in rats.

Sinemet A well-known Parkinson's medication; trade name of combined carbidopa-levodopa.

substantia nigra An area in the upper part of the brain stem that is affected by Parkinson's. Nerve cells in this area of the brain release dopamine into the portion of the brain that controls movement.

task-specific tremor Occurs during highly skilled tasks such as writing or speaking.

thalamotomy Brain surgery that destroys part of the thalamus to relieve severe tremor in advanced Parkinson's disease.

thalamus The gray matter located deep within the brain near the base. This area processes a large portion of the impulses traveling to the brain from the spinal cord and cerebellum.

tremor Involuntary movement and shaking of the body due to muscle contractions associated with Parkinson's.

CHRONOLOGY

B.C.	**5000**	Parkinson's disease–like symptoms are described in an ancient Indian text called *Kampavata*. The symptoms are treated with the tropical legume *Mucuna pruriens*, a natural source of levodopa, which is a drug used to replace dopamine in Parkinson's patients.
	500	An ancient Chinese medical text describes symptoms of Parkinson's disease.
A.D.	**175**	Greek physician Galen describes "shaking palsy."
	1590s	In William Shakespeare's play *The Second Part of King Henry the Sixth*, act 4, scene 7, the character Lord Say states that he has the shaking palsy.
	mid-1600s	Author John Aubrey writes a biography of philosopher Thomas Hobbes and uses the term shaking palsy to describe Hobbes's illness.
	1817	The first scientific description of the disease is written by surgeon James Parkinson in his scientific paper, "An Essay on the Shaking Palsy."
	1828–1835	Physician Wilhelm von Humboldt details his own symptoms of Parkinson's disease.
	1850s	French neurologist Jean-Martin Charcot is the first to refer to Parkinson's disease when he conducts an in-depth study of shaking palsy symptoms.

1880	Charcot completes the first full clinical description of Parkinson's disease, accompanied by drawings.
1886	William Gower publishes his *Manual of Diseases of the Nervous System*.
1892	Rigidity is recognized as one of the most important symptoms of Parkinson's.
early 1900s	Abnormalities in the substantia nigra area of the brain are documented.
1918	An epidemic of *encephalitis lethargica* leaves a large number of people with parkinsonism, characteristics of Parkinson's disease. The epidemic lasts until 1926.
1919	Nigral lesions are found to be constant in Parkinson's patients.
1947	The first stereotactic pallidotomy is performed. In this procedure markers are placed around the head on a frame mounted to the skull and an image is taken with the frame that gives the surgeon reference points for the location of a lesion.
1950	Decreases in dopamine levels are found in Parkinson's patients.
1955	Thalamotomy, brain surgery to destroy part of the thalamus, is introduced to help reduce tremors.
1957	Parkinson's Disease Foundation is founded.

1960s Chemical differences are found in the brains of Parkinson's patients.

1961 Levodopa is first used to treat Parkinson's symptoms.

1967 D-dopa and L-dopa, synthetic versions of naturally occurring amino acids, are successfully used via high-dose oral applications. D-dopa is found to be clinically inactive.

1969 Amantadine, a drug that controls tremors and other Parkinson's symptoms, is first used successfully.

1970s The drug Sinemet is developed by DuPont for treatment of Parkinson's disease.

1979 MPTP-based Parkinson's symptoms, meaning those derived from the injection of an environmental toxin, are first reported.

1982 Muhammad Ali is diagnosed with Parkinson's disease.

1983 Confirmation is given that Pope John Paul II has Parkinson's disease.

1989 Thalamic deep brain stimulation is used to treat tremors.

1995 Subthalamic deep brain stimulation is used to treat all Parkinson's symptoms.

1996 The location of the first gene associated with Parkinson's disease is found through the National Center for Human Genome Research.

2000   The Michael J. Fox Foundation for Parkinson's Research is founded.

2002   An Emory University study finds that laboratory rats develop symptoms similar to Parkinson's disease after receiving injections of the environmental toxin rotenone.

2004   Amgen Inc. halts phase II trials of its Parkinson's drug GDNF, citing potential patient harm.

2005   Studies show that diet may play an important part in the control of early-stage Parkinson's disease.

2006   Biologists develop a technique for establishing colonies of human embryonic stem cells, furthering the controversy over adult versus embryonic stem cells.

2007   Researchers announce that they have found a way to manufacture stem cells from human skin tissue instead of using embryonic cells.

Naturally occurring brain chemicals are found to be similar to chemical compounds found in marijuana and hashish and cause a major improvement in mice with Parkinson's symptoms.

2008   Researchers find that people with Parkinson's disease can identify twenty or fewer smells correctly, while people with a normal sense of smell can identify thirty-five to forty different smells.

ORGANIZATIONS TO CONTACT

The editors have compiled the following list of organizations concerned with the issues debated in this book. The descriptions are derived from the materials provided by the organizations. All have publications or information available for interested readers. The list was compiled on the date of publication of the present volume; the information provided here may change. Be aware that many organizations take several weeks or longer to respond to inquiries, so allow as much time as possible.

American Parkinson Disease Association Inc. (APDA)
135 Parkinson Ave.
Staten Island, NY 10305
(718) 981-8001 or
(800) 223-2732
fax: (718) 981-4399
www.apdaparkinson
.org

This organization focuses on research, patient support, education, and public awareness. It has more than fifty local chapters. APDA has also established the National Young Onset Center to address the needs of young adults afflicted with Parkinson's. The APDA's Web site offers detailed patient information on the medical aspects of Parkinson's.

The Michael J. Fox Foundation for Parkinson's Research
Church St. Station
PO Box 780
New York, NY 10008-0780
(800) 708-7644
www.michaeljfox.org

Founded by actor Michael J. Fox, this national organization funds research and develops therapies for Parkinson's patients. It also offers information on the causes, symptoms, and treatments of Parkinson's and provides guides for caregivers and newly diagnosed patients. Its Web site offers information on research opportunities and programs, Parkinson's news and events, and links to other Parkinson's resources. The organization's print newsletter, *Accelerating the Cure*, is published three times per year and its e-newsletter, *FoxFlash*, is published monthly.

National Parkinson Foundation
1501 NW Ninth Ave.
Bob Hope Rd.
Miami, FL 33136-1494
(305) 243-6666 or
(800) 327-4545
fax: (305) 243-5595
www.parkinson.org

This organization supports Parkinson's research and focuses on education for Parkinson's patients and the general public. The organization also works to improve the quality of life for individuals suffering from Parkinson's disease. A wide variety of free publications dealing with Parkinson's is available by mail or for download, including basic overviews, medications, caregiving, nutrition, fitness, and mental and emotional issues.

Parkinson's Action Network
1025 Vermont Ave.
NW, Ste. 1120
Washington, DC
20005
(202) 638-4101 or
(800) 850-4726
fax: (202) 638-7257
www.parkinsons
action.org

This national advocacy organization focuses on public policy issues involving Parkinson's disease. Local grassroots groups help lobby individual states and government organizations on behalf of Parkinson's. Its Web site offers an extensive listing of links to national and international Parkinson's groups and issues.

Parkinson's Disease Foundation
1359 Broadway
Ste. 1509
New York, NY 10018
(212) 638-4101 or
(800) 457-6676
fax: (212) 923-4478
www.pdf.org

This national organization focuses on research, patient education, and public advocacy. Its Parkinson's Information Service (PINS) offers specialist information and counseling via a toll-free helpline or "Ask the Expert" Web service. Also offered is PDtrials, an educational campaign aimed at spreading awareness of available clinical trial treatments and opportunities.

The Parkinson's Institute and Clinical Center
675 Alamanor Ave.
Sunnyvale, CA
94085-2935
(408) 734-2800
www.parkinsons
institute.org

This West Coast organization conducts research and clinical trials. In addition, Parkinson's Institute Movement Disorders Clinic treats twenty distinct disorders associated with Parkinson's disease. The organization also offers physical therapy, speech therapy, and clinical trial opportunities.

Parkinson's Research Organization
74090 El Paseo
Ste. 102
Palm Desert, CA 92260
(760) 773-5628 or
(877) 775-4111
fax: (760) 773-9803
www.parkinsons
resource.org

This psychological-social group focuses on helping Parkinson's-affected families cope with the five stages of the disease. The organization stresses the need to have long-term insurance coverage in place before any diagnosis is made. Its monthly newsletter *Newsworthy Notes* contains information to help patients understand the long-term care aspects of the disease, and its Web site contains an archive of several years of the newsletter.

FOR FURTHER READING

Books

Jackie Hunt Christensen, *The First Year: Parkinson's Disease.* New York: Marlowe, 2005.

Michael J. Fox, *Lucky Man: A Memoir.* New York: Hyperion, 2002.

Thomas Graboys with Peter Zheutlin, *A Life in the Balance.* New York: Union Square, 2008.

Marian Jahanshahi and C. David Marsden, *Parkinson's Disease: A Self-Help Guide.* New York: Demos Medical, 2000.

Abraham N. Lieberman, *100 Questions & Answers About Parkinson's Disease.* Sudbury, MA: Jones and Bartlett, 2003.

Abraham N. Lieberman and Frank L. Williams, *Parkinson's Disease: The Complete Guide for Patients and Caregivers.* New York: Fireside, 1993.

Jill Marjama-Lyons and Mary J. Shomon, *What Your Doctor May Not Tell You About Parkinson's Disease.* New York: Warner, 2003.

Dwight C. McGoon, *The Parkinson's Handbook.* New York: W.W. Norton, 1990.

Nick Nelson, *Monkeys in the Middle: How One Drug Company Kept a Parkinson's Disease Breakthrough Out of Reach.* Charleston, SC: BookSurge, 2008.

Shelley Peterman Schwartz, *Parkinson's Disease: 300 Tips for Making Life Easier.* New York: Demos Medical, 2006.

Michele Tagliati, Gary N. Guten, and Jo Horne, *Parkinson's Disease for Dummies.* Hoboken, NJ: Wiley, 2007.

Periodicals

Sarah Baldauf, "Beyond Wrinkles," *US News & World Report,* vol. 142, no. 3, January 22, 2007.

Beryl Lieff Bederly, "Experimental Drugs on Trial," *Scientific American*, vol. 297, no. 4, October 2007.

Daniel Bergnew, "A Death in the Family," *New York Times Magazine*, December 2, 2007.

Kyla Dunn, "Stem Cell Setbacks Inspire New Methods," *Discover*, January 2007.

Eric Hagerman, "The Deadly Five," *Popular Science*, vol. 271, no. 4, October 2007.

Jeffrey Kluger, "Rewiring the Brain," *Time*, vol. 170, no. 11, September 10, 2007.

Steven Kotler, "Juicing 3.0," *Popular Science*, vol. 273, no. 2, August 2008.

Scott Rabb, "What I've Learned: Michael J. Fox," *Esquire*, vol. 149, no. 1, January 2008.

Seattle Times, "Stem Cell Developments Are Not Replacements," November 26, 2007.

Matthew Shulman, "When Music Becomes Medicine for the Brain," *US News & World Report*, vol. 145, no. 5, September 1–8, 2008.

Lee M. Silver, "Half Human, Half Cow, All Baloney," *Newsweek*, May 12, 2008.

Roslyn Sulcas, "Getting Their Groove Back, with Help from the Magic of Dance," *New York Times*, August 25, 2007.

Kaylee Thompson, "Diagnosis 2.0," *Popular Science*, vol. 271, no. 6, December 2007.

US News & World Report, "Gene Linked to Form of Parkinson's Disease," March 21, 2008.

Adam Voiland, "Low LDL Cholesterol Levels Linked to Parkinson's Disease," *US News & World Report*, December 19, 2006.

Internet Sources

Associated Press, "Gene Therapy Offers Hope for Easing Parkinson's," MSNBC.com, June 21, 2007. www.msnbc.msn .com/id/19355047.

Mike Celizic, "Michael J. Fox Isn't Letting Disease Define Him," MSNBC.com, December 3, 2007. www.msnbc.msn.com/id/22080118.

Maggie Fox, "Clone Cells Treat Parkinson's in Mice," Reuters, June 21, 2008. www.michaeljfox.org/news.

Robert A. Hauser, "Parkinson's Disease," May 17, 2007. www.emedicine.com/neuro/TOPIC304.htm.

HealthLink, "The Facts About Parkinson's Disease," Medical College of Wisconsin, July 8, 2003. http://healthlink.mcw.edu/article/1031002268.html.

Medical News Today, "AMT Obtains License to Amgen's GDNF Gene to Develop Treatment for Parkinson's Disease with AMT's Proprietary Gene Therapy Platform," September 27, 2008. www.medicalnewstoday.com/articles/123283.php.

————— "Neurologix Initiates Recruitment for Phase 2 Parkinson's Disease Trial," August 24, 2008. www.medicalnewstoday.com/articles/118912.php.

————— "Surgical Technique Halts Cell Loss, Parkinson's Researchers Find," September 4, 2008. www.medicalnewstoday.com/articles/120193.php.

Michael S. Okun, "What's 'Red Hot' in PD? Exciting Developments on the Horizon for PD," National Parkinson's Foundation, January 9, 2008. www.parkinson.org.

ScienceDaily, "Identification of Dopamine 'Mother Cells' Could Lead to Future Parkinson's Treatments," April 9, 2008. www.sciencedaily/com/releases/2008/04/080407114604.htm.

INDEX